In the name of Allah, the Most Gracious, the Most Merciful

Economic Success

Practical Strategies for Producing Wealth and Combating Poverty in the System of Imam Ali

Translated from the original Arabic written by

Sayed Mortadha al-Husayni al-Shirazi

Economic Success: Practical Strategies for Producing Wealth and Combating Poverty in the System of Imam Ali

Written by Sayed Mortadha al-Husayni al-Shirazi
Edited by Arifa Hudda

ISBN: 978-09910250-2-2

Cover Design and Layout by Islamic Publishing House - www.iph.ca

Published by Imam Jaafar al-Sadeq Center
yasahibalzaman@gmail.com

Contents

Preface[1]

All praise is due to Allah, the Lord of the Worlds, and may His peace and blessings be upon the trustworthy Messenger of Allah, Muhammad, and his noble family - the Ahlulbayt. May Allah's curse also be upon their enemies until the Day of Judgment. There is no power or might except by Allah, the Sublime, the Mighty.

Almighty Allah states in the Holy Quran:

> He brought you forth from the earth and settled you therein.[2]

Allah the Exalted also states:

> Observe fully the measure and the balance with justice and diminish not people's goods, and behave not wickedly upon the earth, engaged in corruption.[3]

---

[1] This book is a compilation of a series of lectures delivered by Ayatollah Sayed Mortadha al-Shirazi at the Sixth Imam Ali (a) Conference hosted by Al-Ferdows World Center for Media and Culture. The conference was held at Porchester Hall in London, UK on the occasion of the birth of Imam Ali (a) which fell around the 13th of Rajab, 1427 AH (August 5, 2006). Later, the author edited and revised the book, in addition to adding new chapters such as chapter four.

[2] *Quran*, Surah Hud (11), verse 61.

[3] Ibid., verse 85.

In yet another verse, He states:

> He it is who created for you all that is in the earth.[4]

Imam Ali (a) said:

> If poverty was to be embodied before me in the form of a human being, I would kill him.[5]

Before addressing this very important and lively topic, we must offer an introduction that will define poverty and refer to the limits of poverty, the extent of poverty, poverty areas, and the types of poverty in the words of Imam Ali (a).

We will also address why we chose Imam Ali (a) and his teachings to be our guide and role model in this discussion.

What is Poverty?

In order for us to know how big of a problem poverty is, we must first come to know the correct and complete meaning of poverty.

Contrary to what most people assume, poverty is not restricted to the materialistic dimension. Poverty extends to many other fields and dimensions because the essence of poverty is need and deprivation. Need and deprivation are the common denominators which are found in all of the definitions of poverty.

Therefore, poverty encompasses all of the following examples:

1. **Deprivation of love and emotions.** One narration states: "Isn't religion anything other than love?"[6] Another narration states: "Have mercy upon those who are on the earth, and those who are in the heavens will have mercy on you."[7] A line in one of the supplications (*Du'a Kumayl*) reads: "And through Your

---

[4] *Quran*, Surah al-Baqarah (2), verse 29.

[5] *Rawa'e' Nahj al-Balagha* by George Jordac, p. 84 and p. 233; *Sharh Ihqaq al-Haqq*, vol. 32, p. 213.

[6] This narration is attributed to Imam al-Sadiq (a). Refer to *al-Kafi*, vol. 2, p. 125.

[7] This narration is attributed to Prophet Muhammad (s). Refer to *Mustadrak al-Wasa'il*, vol. 9, p. 55, trad. 8.

greatness You extend Your compassion towards me."[8]

2. **Deprivation of proper education.** This type of deprivation includes religious and worldly sciences. Allah the Almighty states in the Holy Quran: "...(He - the Prophet) purifies them and teaches them the Book and the Wisdom."[9]

3. **Deprivation of proper and complete healthcare.** This type of deprivation includes the well-being of the body, soul and the intellect. A narration states: "The sciences are four ... and the science of medicine is for the protection of the bodies."[10]

4. **Deprivation of proper physical exercise** and the practice of sports which a human being needs to maintain the well-being of their body, soul and intellect. This is why certain sports are recommended in Islam, such as swimming, archery and horseback riding.

5. **Deprivation of proper housing** that fulfills one's physical, spiritual and psychological needs. One narration states: "(A source) of good fortune for a Muslim is to have a spacious residence."[11]

6. **Deprivation of proper clothing.** Allah the Almighty states in the Holy Quran: "Attend to your beautiful apparel,"[12] and in another verse He states: "O Children of Adam, We have indeed bestowed upon you clothing to cover your shame and (clothing) for beauty."[13]

7. **Deprivation of food and water.** A human being needs food and water to secure his required caloric intake and vital

[8] Du'a Kumayl by Imam Ali (a) as found in *al-Misbah*, p. 560.

[9] *Quran*, Surah al-Jumu'ah (62), verse 2.

[10] *Sharh Resalat al-Huquq* (the Treatise on Rights) by Imam Ali ibn al-Husayn Zain al-Abidin (a), p. 385.

[11] *Al-Kafi*, vol. 6, p. 526.

[12] *Quran*, Surah al-A'raf (7), verse 31.

[13] Ibid., verse 26.

vitamins and proteins. Allah states in the Holy Quran: "So let them worship the Lord of this House; Who feeds them against hunger."[14] In another verse, Allah states: "and the good provisions."[15]

8. **Being deprived of a vehicle for transportation**. A narration states: "A source of good fortune for a person ... is (to have) a fast mode of transportation."[16]

9. **Being deprived of ornaments, adornments and luxuries.** Allah states: "Say: Who has prohibited the adornments of Allah which He has brought forth for His servants?"[17]

There are other types and dimensions of poverty that may be much more serious than those mentioned above. Some of them include:

1. **Being deprived of social, political and economic security.** Allah the Almighty states: "And gave them security against fear."[18] Fear includes anything that threatens the human being socially, economically and politically. Allah also says: "And removes from them their burden and the shackles which were upon them."[19] The verse is a reference to the burdens and shackles which Prophet Muhammad (s) removed and destroyed. He removed the barriers that limited the freedom of trade, farming, production and transportation, including those barriers that were a product of local customs and culture.

2. **Being deprived of primary and secondary rights**, such

---

[14] *Quran*, Surah al-Quraysh (106), verses 3-4.

[15] *Quran*, Surah al-A'raf (7), verse 32.

[16] *Al-Fiqh: Al-Idara* (The Law of Management) by the late Imam Shirazi, vol. 2, p. 176, 1992 edition.

[17] *Quran*, Surah al-A'raf (7), verse 32.

[18] *Quran*, Surah al-Quraysh (106), verse 4.

[19] *Quran*, Surah al-A'raf (7), verse 157.

as the right to freedom of expression, the right to travel or stay home, the right to own property, the right to conduct business, the right to invest,[20] and thousands of other rights. The basis of these rights is found in religious rulings such as the narration of Prophet Muhammad (s) which states: "People have authority over themselves and their wealth."[21] Other religious rulings include the verse of the Quran which states: "The Prophet has a greater claim on the faithful than they have on themselves,"[22] the Prophetic tradition which states: "There is no harm or harming (in Islam),"[23] and the verse of the Quran which states: "You shall have your religion, and I shall have my religion."[24]

3. **Being deprived of sound ideas, proper intellectual engagements, and correct beliefs.** Allah the Almighty states: "And We indeed gave Abraham his sound judgment (rectitude);"[25] and in another verse of the Quran, He states: "(He - the Prophet) purifies them and teaches them the Book and the Wisdom."[26]

4. **Being deprived of economic and political independence.**

Poverty is not confined to an individual, as it also includes the

---

[20] Refer to the books *al-Fiqh: al-Hurriyaat* and *al-Fiqh: al-Huquq* by the late Grand Ayatollah Sayed Muhammad Shirazi.

[21] *Al-Khilaf*, by Shaykh al-Tousi, vol. 3, p. 176.

[22] *Quran*, Surah al-Ahzab (33), verse 6. Since Allah Has granted the Prophet (s) utmost authority, he has greater authority over us than we have over ourselves. Hence, when Allah says in this verse that the Prophet (s) has a greater claim on the faithful than they have on themselves, it means that people have a claim on themselves, otherwise it would not make sense to say the Prophet (s) has a greater claim on us if we had no claim on ourselves.

[23] *Al-Kafi*, vol. 5, p. 280.

[24] *Quran*, Surah al-Kafirun (109), verse 6.

[25] *Quran*, Surah al-Anbiya' (21), verse 51.

[26] *Quran*, Surah al-Jumu'ah (62), verse 2.

poverty of a society and the poverty of a government. Just as poverty is applicable to a poor individual, it also applies to a government that lacks constitutional institutions, and it also applies to a government and a society which lack proper infrastructure.[27 and 28]

Imam Ali (a) and Poverty Areas

The narrations and teachings of Imam Ali (a) reflect the comprehensive dimensions and aspects of poverty.

1. As for intellectual (or educational) poverty, Imam Ali (a)

---

[27] Refer to the book *Ma'alem al-Mojtama al-Madani fi Mandhoomatil Fikril Islami* by the author.

[28] Poverty is defined as not being able to meet the minimum level of basic material needs such as food, shelter, clothing, education and health. It also includes non-material needs such as the right of participation, individual freedom, and social justice. Poverty is also defined as not being able to meet the minimum standard of living. It is possible to define poor countries as those countries which suffer from inadequate standards in education, healthcare, access to clean and healthy water for human consumption and sanitation, and access to proper nutrition in terms of quantity and quality for each member of society, in addition to undergoing a continued state of loss and deterioration of its natural resources and the expansion of poverty areas.

The World Bank has defined poor countries as those countries in which the annual income (or GDP) for each person falls below $600. There are 45 such countries, many of which are in Africa, and in 15 of these countries, the annual income for each person falls below $300.

As for the United Nations Development Program, it added multiple other factors that determine economic comfort and sustainable livelihoods. According to this definition which expanded the meaning of poverty to include the quality of life as well, seventy countries are considered poor, meaning that 45% of poor people are living in societies which do not fall below the poverty life if we consider the GDP only, but they are poor when we consider their quality of life. Hence, there are many poor people living in rich countries, and it suffices to mention here that 30 million Americans (which is about 15% of the population) in the United States fall below the poverty line.

states: "There is no wealth like knowledge, and there is no poverty like ignorance."[29] Ignorance is essentially intellectual, educational and cultural poverty. Ignorance is also one of the primary causes of economic poverty.

2. Imam Ali (a) also makes a reference to poverty and being deprived of education, awareness and sound intellect by his statement: "The biggest poverty is stupidity (or foolishness)."[30]

3. As for being deprived of political and social security and safety, the Imam (a) states: "Neither are you a support for me to lean upon, nor (*zawafer*) a means to honor and victory."[31] The word '*zawafer*' in Arabic is the plural form of the word '*zaferah*' which if used to describe a building, refers to its foundation; if it is used to describe a person, then it means his family and supporters. This type of poverty includes individual poverty, state poverty, and social poverty.

4. Imam Ali (a) also makes a reference to spiritual and moral poverty by saying: "The worst type of poverty is the poverty of the soul."[32] In another narration he states: "The biggest tribulation is the poverty of the soul."[33] In a third narration, the Imam (a) makes a general statement which applies to this type of poverty as well. He says: "There may be a poor person who is richer than every rich person."[34] This type of poverty has many examples, such as the poverty of health, security and rights. There may be a poor person who is poor financially, but when considering his health, he is rich. There may also be a rich person who is financially rich, but his wealth is incapable of providing him with good health and

---

[29] *Nahj al-Balagha*, vol. 4, p. 14, maxim 54.

[30] Ibid., vol. 4, p. 11, maxim 38.

[31] Ibid., sermon 34.

[32] *Ghurar al-Hikam*, p. 232.

[33] Ibid.

[34] Ibid. p. 366.

well-being. There may be a rich person who is wealthy, but he is poor in terms of his primary and secondary rights, such as the right to freedom of expression, the right to travel, the right to own property and the right to invest. Such a wealthy person is in a worse state than the one who is financially poor, but he is rich in having rights.

5. Imam Ali (a) makes a reference to religious and ideological poverty by saying: "Poverty is to be a loser in both worlds" (this life and the hereafter).[35] In this statement, poverty means to be deprived of religion, piety, being mindful of God, morality and ethics—all of which cause one to be a loser in this life and in the hereafter. The one who suffers from religious poverty will not restrain himself from committing certain sins or crimes, such as robbery, murder and other crimes. Likewise, a government that lacks a moral and religious deterrent will constrict freedoms of the people, will imprison free and innocent people, and will repress the majority and the minority. This is indeed a loss in both of the worlds!

6. There is a verse in the Holy Quran which captures the words of Prophet Moses (a) when he addressed Allah and said to Him: "My Lord, I am in need of whatever good that You may send down to me."[36] When considering the context of this verse's revelation, we see that it is referring to food, as Prophet Moses (a) was extremely hungry when he made this prayer. However, the generality of this prayer includes all types of needs, since the human being is in need of all types of favors from God in each and every matter of their lives.

7. Imam Ali (a) says: "The poorest person is the one who is parsimonious (or cheap) with himself even though he is

[35] *Awali al-Liyali*, vol. 1, p. 40.

[36] *Quran*, Surah al-Qasas (28), verse 24.

wealthy, and he bequeaths his wealth to someone else."[37] Poverty does not mean that one does not own money or wealth; rather, it means that one deprives himself from benefiting from his wealth and using it to meet his various needs, such as: material and spiritual, political and social, educational and cultural, and his basic, essential and non-essential needs. Hence, the one who possesses billions but does not utilize it to fight for one's rights and the rights of his nation is a poor person, and indeed he is the poorest of the poor. Similarly, a country that owns hundreds of billions but does not invest them in its infrastructure and in empowering its constitutional institutions is a poor country indeed.

Indeed, there is only one type of good and beneficial poverty, which is essentially the pinnacle of richness, and that is being in need of Allah the Almighty. One supplication reads: "O Allah, enrich me by impoverishing me to You, and do not impoverish me by making me not need You."[38] There is another supplication in the Book of Prophet Idris (a) which says: "There is no richness for the one who does not need You; and there is no poverty for the one who needs You."[39]

Poverty: the Greatest Challenge

Poverty is considered among the greatest challenges that humanity has faced throughout history. Poverty, along with ignorance, disease, and lack of safety, comprise the four corners of human misery and backwardness.

Despite our modern technological advancements, and despite the economic programs and planning that we have, whether at the local or international level, poverty continues to be the greatest concern for humanity, and poses the greatest danger to humanity. A report released by the President of the World Bank

---

[37] *Ghurar al-Hikam*, p. 369.

[38] *Bihar al-Anwar*, vol. 69, p. 31. Also see *Safinah al-Bihar*, vol. 8, p. 272.

[39] Ibid., vol. 95, p. 462.

states:

> Out of six billion people, 2.8 billion live on less than $2.00 a day, and 1.2 billion live on less than $1.00 per day. Out of every 100 infants, six infants die before reaching one year of age. As for children who reach the age of learning, from 100 children, only nine boys and fourteen girls are able to attend elementary school, and the rest stay behind their doors.[40]

The problem of poverty is quite complicated and it is intertwined with all other aspects of life—the political, social, psychological, intellectual, spiritual, legal and religious aspects of life. Since poverty has a mutual or reciprocal relationship with each of these aspects, each aspect plays a role in creating the problem of poverty, and in turn, it is also affected by poverty.

Therefore, it has become evident that human beings are incapable of arriving at a complete and comprehensive solution to the problem of poverty.[41]

If there is a fundamental solution to this problem, then it must

[40] Every several years, the World Bank releases updated reports on the conditions of poverty based on the latest global data concerning the cost of living and regional surveys on average household consumption. The estimates released by the World Bank on February 29th, 2012 indicate that those who live on less than $1.25 a day reached about 1.29 billion people in 2008. This represents 22% of the population of the developing world. The updated report relies on 850 household surveys conducted in about 130 countries.

[41] According to an old survey, there are more than 6 billion people living on earth. The population of developing countries is 4.3 billion, and about 3 billion of them live below the line of poverty, which is $2.00 per day. Among them, some 1.2 billion people live on less than $1.00 per day. Nearly half of the world's population today live in cities and towns. In 2005, nearly one-third (1 billion people) lived in the straps of poverty. In developing countries, we find that 33.3% do not have access to safe or clean water suitable for drinking or other uses, 25% lack proper housing, 20% lack the most basic and normal health services, 20% of children do not make it past the fifth grade, 20% of students

come from a Divine source, since the Wise, Just, Omniscient, All-Encompassing and Omnipotent Lord is the One who has a solution to this problem, and the solution is comprised of these three components: humanity, resources, and the system or strategy.

It is for this reason that we commenced our endeavor to find the solution to the problem of poverty by referring to the Divine teachings contained in the Holy Quran and found in the words of Prophet Muhammad (s) and Imam Ali (a).

Why have we Chosen Imam Ali (a) as a Teacher, Guide, and Instructor?

The following factors are why we primarily chose the words, teachings and actions of Imam Ali (a) in the field of economics as the basis for arriving at strategic solutions to combat poverty:

1. Imam Ali (a) is the most familiar with the path of God after Prophet Muhammad (s). The Prophet (s) said: "The most knowledgeable amongst you is Ali."[42]
2. Imam Ali (a) passed down to us in his narrations, words, speeches and especially his treatise to Malik al-Ashtar[43] broad guidelines that depict for us a very clear strategy to combat poverty throughout history.
3. Imam Ali (a) experienced firsthand the daily struggles of poverty, since he was born into a poor society, and he tasted poverty, so he was fully aware of the pain of poverty.
4. Imam Ali (a) was distinguished by his vast experience and great expertise in dealing with poverty. He was with the Prophet (s) and witnessed both the days of severe poverty and

---

suffer from malnutrition, and about 30,000 children die daily due to poverty.

[42] *Al-Kafi*, vol. 7, p. 424.

[43] The complete text of this document is presented at the end of this book. (Tr.)

also the days in which wealth began pouring in to the Prophet (s). He learned from the Prophet (s) how to deal with poverty, how to deal with wealth, and how to utilize the wealth in creating a comprehensive strategy to combat poverty.

5. Imam Ali (a) used his personal experiences with lifelong difficulties and translated those experiences into practical measures to combat poverty. When he got married, he lived the life of the poor with his beloved wife, the pure and truthful Fatima al-Zahra (a). Sometimes he would pawn his armor so he could borrow three kilograms of barley for the day.[44] The Imam (s) would also work very hard in farming and in trade. Then when the wealth began pouring in during

[44] Scholars have narrated that the eighth verse of Surah al-Insaan (76): "And they give food out of love for Him to the poor and the orphan and the captive," and the ninth verse of the same chapter: "We only feed you for Allah's sake; we desire from you neither reward nor thanks," were revealed in honor of the Ahlulbayt (a).

Imam Hasan (a) and Husayn (a) became ill, so Prophet Muhammad (s) visited them and then Imam Ali (a), Lady Fatima (a) and their maid, Fiddha, made a vow to fast for three days if they recover. When they recovered from their sickness, Imam Ali (a) borrowed about six kilograms of barley because they had absolutely nothing at home.

Fatima (a) ground two kilograms and baked a loaf of bread for each one of them. Imam Ali (a) performed the *maghrib* prayer and then came home when the food was presented before him. A destitute came and asked them for food, so each of them offered him their loaf. They spent that day and night without eating anything.

They fasted the following day and Fatima (a) baked another two kilograms of flour into bread, and when she put the loaves in front of them, an orphan came and asked them for food. All of them offered their loaves as charity to him.

After fasting the third day, and when they were about to break their fast, a captive came and asked them for some food, so they all offered him their loaves of bread. Thus, they did not consume anything during those three days of fasting, except for water.

The Prophet (s) saw them on the fourth day while they were shaking from hunger, and Fatima's stomach had become attached to her back

his caliphate, he implemented his strategies in combating poverty, especially in the areas of social security and public welfare. He used all of the resources at his disposal to combat poverty.[45]

6. Imam Ali (a) was distinguished by his exceptional perseverance and mighty willpower in presenting exemplary solutions to poverty. A significant step he took towards combating poverty was that he cultivated very vast lands around the city of Medina by taking advantage of the twenty-five years in which he was marginalized for his opposition to the dictatorship that ensued after the death of Prophet Muhammad (a) and the abandonment of his teachings. Through his actions, he taught people to work and produce for themselves rather than waiting for others to help them.[46]

7. Imam Ali (a) was a shining star, theoretically and practically,

---

due to excessive hunger, and her eyes had sunken in. The Prophet (s) said: "Help us, O Allah! The family of Muhammad die of hunger?!"

The angel Gabriel descended and said to him: "Take what Allah has blessed you with for your family."

The Prophet (s) said to him: "What do I take, O Gabriel?" He read to him Sura al-Insaan.

Refer to the following sources: *Shawahid al-Tanzil* by al-Hakem al-Hasakani, vol. 2, pp. 393-414, trad. no. 1042-1070; *Manaqib al-Maghazili*, p. 272, trad. no. 320; *Asbaab al-Nuzul* by al-Wahidi, p. 296; *Al-Durr al-Manthour* by al-Soyouti, vol. 8, p. 371; *Dhakha'er al-Uqba*, p. 102; *Tafsir al-Baydhawi*, vol. 5, p. 165; *Tafsir al-Tabari*, vol. 29, p. 125; *Tasfir al-Fakhr al-Razi*, vol. 30, p. 243; *Al-Kashhaf* by al-Zamakhshari, vol. 4, p. 670; *Sharh Nahj al-Balagha* by Ibn Abil Hadid, vol. 1, p. 21; *Ihqaaq al-Haqq* by al-Tostari, vol. 3, pp. 158-196, and vol. 9, pp. 110-123; *Fadha'il al-Khamsa min al-Sihah al-Sitta*, vol. 1, p. 301.

[45] Refer to the book *Public Welfare in Islam* and also *Politics from an Islamic Viewpoint* by the Grand Ayatollah Sayed Sadeq al-Husayni al-Shirazi.

[46] In the book *Politics from an Islamic Viewpoint*, the Grand Ayatollah Sayed Sadeq al-Husayni al-Shirazi states: "Islam adopted a wise policy in increasing development and farming, and it is through these two

> when he became the ruler of the Islamic government—a government on which the sun almost never set during that time. He came forth with a comprehensive economic theory and he implemented it, thereby transforming his society into a paradise where no poor person was to be found. He accomplished this in less than five years, such that he says: "It may be possible that in Hejaz or Yamama there is someone who has no hope of obtaining a piece of bread and has never satisfied his hunger."[47]

Historians have also mentioned that in Africa, not a single poor person (who would go hungry) was to be found.[48]

The treatise of Imam Ali (a) to Malik al-Ashtar (which can

---

that a government either rises or falls. Islam made lands available to anyone who would develop them by either building on them, using them for farming, creating water channels, and starting water springs in them; or among other uses, constructing factories on them. Islam encouraged people to work, farm, and build expansive homes. It has been narrated that Prophet Muhammad (s) said: 'Whoever develops a dead land (undeveloped land that does not belong to anyone), then it belongs to him, and as for the one who oppresses (usurps land from others, or farms in land that does not belong to him), then he has no right.'"

[47] Yamama is a region south of the Hejaz on the Arabian Peninsula. The expression "it may be possible" is an Arabic expression which means "there isn't."

[48] The Late Grand Ayatollah Sayed Muhammad al-Husayni al-Shirazi states: "The Commander of the Faithful Imam Ali (a) provided shelter, water and sustenance for all of his nation, even though he ruled over vast territories which spanned nearly fifty countries on today's map. The territories he ruled included Egypt, Hejaz, Yemen, Iran, the Gulf, Iraq and others. Hence, his government was the largest government in the world back then, yet he was able to provide all of those needs for his nation through his wise means of government. Imam Ali (a) achieved that by fully implementing the laws of Islam. For example, one Islamic law states: 'Land belongs to Allah and to the one who develops it.' Imam Ali (a) would offer people land for free, then he would help them build and develop those lands from the

be found at the end of this book) reflects one dimension of his extraordinary economic strategy or plan in combating poverty.

In the following chapters and sections of this book, some features of the foundations Imam Ali (a) laid out in solving the problem of poverty and some features of his everlasting strategy will be presented.

---

treasury. Furthermore, trade, production and farming were all free during his government, and in addition to the money that he would distribute among people from the treasury, people would benefit from various methods of earning a lawful living. People were also free to dig up wells and channels to obtain water, without having to pay any taxes or acquiring any permits. Through these methods, the Imam (a) managed to provide water, shelter and sustenance for all of his nation, a feat that Western nations have not been able to achieve despite their claims of reaching the peak of civilization in our time. In the government of Imam Ali (a), unemployment was not an issue because every person had the opportunity to make a lawful living, and there was a not a single poor person in the vast territories which he ruled over, such that the Imam (a) said: 'It may be possible that in Hejaz or Yamama there is someone who has no hope of obtaining a piece of bread and has never satisfied his hunger.' The Imam uses the word "*la'alla*" in Arabic which means "maybe" or "possibly" because he is hinting that there is no poor person in his nation in the sense that he, the leader of this vast nation, was not sure that there was even a single poor person." Refer to the book, *Fatima al-Zahra (a) the Best Role Model for Women.*

Chapter One

Economic and Religious Factors related to Producing Wealth, Conserving it, and Developing it, and the Primary Causes of Wasting Resources and Creating Poverty and Deprivation

Section One

Economic Factors for Producing Wealth, Conserving it, Developing it, and Combating Poverty

Strategic Solutions[49]

The strategic solutions in combating poverty are divided into two types:

The first type is preventive solutions. These types of solutions aim at preventing the creation of poverty. More specifically, these types of solutions focuses on the factors which create wealth, conserve wealth, and develop wealth. These factors are tied to the infrastructure, the grounds and the general programs

[49] We borrowed the term "strategic solutions" from its military usage, and by it we mean the quality, long-term solutions, whether pursuing these solutions is the responsibility of the government, the responsibility of civil institutions, or responsibility shared by all. This will be evident by examining the fourteen terms which will be laid out.

which breed or foster poverty.

The second type is corrective (or diagnostic) solutions. These types of solutions aim at treating the problem of poverty once it has occurred.

We will examine the first type of solutions in this chapter and in the second chapter; and we will examine the second type of solutions in chapter three, God-Willing.

It is important to note that some preventive factors which prevent the creation of poverty can also be considered as corrective factors which aid in eliminating poverty once it has occurred. Some factors are capable of achieving both.

For example, there is one factor that both impedes the creation of wealth and also perpetuates, continues and deepens the problem of poverty - this factor is the governments' ownership of lands, minerals, and resources, or its control over them such that people are not allowed to benefit from them or assume possession of them, except by applying for permits which involves a complicated process and conditions that are difficult to meet.

For this reason, we have examined this factor—which is making lands and public resources available to all people, instead of the government hoarding or monopolizing them—in chapters one and three, although we have worded it differently in each chapter. We will examine this factor in both chapters due to its critical role in both preventing poverty and also treating it once it has occurred.

It is important to note that all of the factors which will be mentioned in the following three chapters will be divided according to the below manner:

1. Individual/personal factors: These are factors which are influenced by individuals - such as gambling, usury, wasting resources, squandering wealth, paying charity, maintaining ties with one's relatives, and so on.
2. Governmental factors: These are concerned with a

government's laws, system of governance and economic management, and the way in which it controls its resources and deals with the poor and the rich. Some examples are the government's right of ownership, government theft, high number of governmental employees, militarization, lack of proper distribution, maintaining a balance between rural and urban areas, being flexible with taxes, and so on.

3. Factors which are concerned with both the government and the people: Some examples are rationing or cutting back on spending, social security, welfare, piety, honesty, financial corruption, monopolization, and counterfeit money.[50]

Yes, when we discuss each of these points, we may not refer to the two sides of the issue. The wise and the intelligent however, will figure that out.

It is also important to note that in regard to the factors concerning the government, people and civil institutions should not simply take a negative stance against the government. Instead, they should strategically pressure the government to change those (unjust or inappropriate) laws, and the methods of executing them, just as we have described in detail in our book about the state and its citizens,[51] and also in our other book about civil society.[52]

My late father, may Allah shower his soul with mercy, has also explained this in detail in a number of his books.[53]

---

[50] A government may practice monopolization, or people may practice it. Also, people may counterfeit money, or a government may print money more than its economy can handle or more than the reserves that it has. We also consider this a type of counterfeiting or forgery.

[51] The title of the book in Arabic is *Malameh al-Ilaqa bayn al-Dawlah wa al-Sha'ab.*

[52] The title of the book in Arabic is *Ma'alem al-Mujtama' al-Madani fi Mandhoomat al-Fikr al-Islami.*

[53] Such as his books *al-Siyagha al-Jadida, al-Sabil ila Inhadh al--Muslimeen, Mumarast al-Taghyeer, al-Fiqh al-Siyasa wa al-Iqtisad, al-*

Factors in Producing Wealth, Preserving Wealth, or Development of Wealth, and Strategies to Combat Poverty

First: Granting All Land, Minerals and Resources to the People[54]

With respect to this first factor, there must be no restrictions or conditions, and in doing so we are holding on to the wisdom of the Almighty Allah and His engineering of our lives, for He has made the earth and that which it contains for His servants. Allah states in the Holy Quran:

> It is He who created for you all that is in the earth.[55]

This means that all of the resources that the earth contains belong to the people; hence, the government does not own the lands and the minerals, the oceans and the environments. They belong to the people, and they have the complete freedom to own and develop them.

Whoever lays their hands on something (such as an unowned piece of land or extracts minerals from the earth), will then own it. The responsibility of the government is simply to oversee the process by which people own these lands or resources (so that people do not violate each other's rights).

Therefore, in order for a poor person to own a home, he does

Huquq, al-Dawlah, and a number of other books.

[54] The word "grant" here is used figuratively and is not to be taken literally because land and all resources have been created by God for the people. Hence, the government does not have to grant them to the people in order for them to own them. People can simply possess them either by laying their hands on them (in accordance with Islamic law), or by developing them (such as developing a piece of unowned land). Refer to the book *al-Fiqh Ihyaa' al-Mawat,* vol. 80, for further legal details.

[55] Quran, Surah al-Baqarah (2) verse 29.

not need to purchase a piece of land, for the holy Prophet (s) said:

> Land belongs to Allah and whoever develops it.

This poor person can simply lay his hands on an unowned piece of land to own it, and must only bear the cost of building upon it.

This article of Islamic law has a profound impact on dealing a severe blow to unemployment, inflation and the rise in the cost of living. This is because land and building material such as brick and wood would be freely available to people so they can build homes, factories, stores, businesses, or develop farmlands and pastures. This will create huge work opportunities and increase the ability of the poor to make investments.

When the poor do not have to pay the government to develop farmlands or pastures, then land and a part of the capital needed to develop a farmland or pasture to breed chicken, sheep and cows, in addition to other business projects will be freely available to those with limited income. The same applies to constructing a factory. One will not need to come up with the money to buy a piece of land or buy some building material, as all that will be freely available to a person, for one can extract the materials that are needed from the mountains, the trees of the forests, and from the earth's minerals as much as one needs.

This is the approach that Imam Ali (a) adopted in his vast and far-reaching government. Land was freely available to all people, and so were the forests. The "*anfal*,"[56] which is a term in Islamic law that refers to the banks of the rivers, the shores of the oceans, the peaks of the mountains, and the interiors of the

---

[56] The word '*anfal*' in Arabic is the plural form of the word '*nafl*,' which means an increase or an addition. For this reason the daily recommended prayers are called '*nawafil*,' as they are additional prayers to the mandatory prayers. This word is also used to describe a gift or grant. Both meanings are quite similar. This term has been used in the holy verse to refer to the goods that are taken from non-Muslim lands (*Dar al-Harb*) without any battle. In a narration, Imam al-Baqir (a) defines '*anfal*' as "minerals, forests, every land that has no owner or every land whose owners have perished."

valleys, were freely available to all people. All they had to do was make the effort to build, farm, develop and invest without paying a single penny to buy what Allah essentially created for them. They were not even subject to routine legal regulations, nor did they have to pay any taxes for simply building a house, factory or farm. Afterall, doesn't Allah say:

> It is He who created for you all that is on the earth.

There is another factor that follows this first factor, and that is granting people the right to invest in public places, and we will make a brief reference to that here.

Granting People the Right to Invest in Public Places

It has been narrated that Imam al-Sadiq (a) said that the Commander of the Faithful (Imam Ali (a)) said:

> 'The market of Muslims is just like their mosque, therefore whoever is first to claim a spot there has a greater right to it until nighttime.' And he would not charge rent for the rooms of the market.[57]

The market is among the shared spaces, meaning that it is an open public space where every human being has the right to work and conduct business. Everyone has the right to choose any place in the market as long as no one claimed it before him. Then, one can use that spot to buy and sell, seal contracts and do business. Only if this law—the law of being free in making use of markets—was to be applied, in addition to the freedom in making use of other public places such as public parks, public water taken from oceans, rivers, natural springs, ponds, oases, public pastures, minerals, and public roads, such that the passersby are not harmed, then there would be many work opportunities for people. In turn, this would become a factor in mitigating and confining poverty in its spheres and areas.

---

[57] *Al-Kafi*, vol. 5, p. 155, trad. 1.

Second: Priority for the Development, Enhancement, and Investment in Infrastructure

This is a law which Imam Ali (a) legislated, as he gave absolute priority for construction, development and production, instead of giving priority to taxation.[58]

We find this law in the treatise of Imam Ali (a) to Malik al-Ashtar when he appointed him as the governor of Egypt. It reads:

> Let your concern about developing the land be greater than your concern about levying taxes.[59]

Then the Imam (a) states the reasoning behind this recommendation, and this reveals the Imam's sharp and strategic vision and his comprehensive economic outlook. The Imam (a) continues to say:

> For you will not achieve that (levying taxes) except through development, and whoever demands taxes without development will ruin the lands and destroy the people, and his reign will not last except a little.[60]

This is where governments make a mistake by focusing on taxes twice. The first is when they destroy the ability of farmers and small investors to produce, leading to an increase in the proportion of poor people. This negatively impacts the government because the amount of taxes which the government levies will certainly decrease. The second is because focusing on taxes will "destroy the people." These powerful word by Imam Ali (a) is evident in

---

[58] Taxation is an amount of money a government levies from individuals and institutions in order to pay government expenses. This means funding all of the sectors which the government spends on, such as education embodied in schools and the wages of the teachers, ministries and their wages, waste management workers, economic policies such as subsidizing products and specific sectors, or spending on infrastructure such as the construction of roads, dams, or unemployment insurance.

[59] *Nahj al-Balagha*, vol. 3, p. 96.

[60] Ibid.

the following phenomena or conditions:

1. Social mayhem may lead to violent and chaotic revolutions that destroy every aspect of society, and it could further worsen the economic conditions.[61]

2. The emergence of diseases that come as a result of psychological stress that farmers and small investors are faced with. This is caused by the government's insistence on levying taxes. Diseases also emerge because such people will lack the ability to secure the necessities of life with peace of mind, and these diseases in turn will cause further poverty and deprivation.

3. The ability of the poor and those with limited income to have access to education will shrink, and their ability to lead a dignified life will also diminish. All of this will have negative consequences on the economy.

4. The most prominent economic experts in development have discovered that if the average rate of investment reaches 25% or 30% of the gross domestic product (GDP) for several consecutive years, this will end recession because the economy will take off. The World Bank also believes that a surge in investments and wealth can solve the problem.[62] Imam Ali (a) was aware of this solution more than 1,350 years before these experts, and in addition to that, the Imam's system was much more advanced, as the Imam (a) did not limit investments to 25% or 30%. Rather he left the door wide open for investing in infrastructure, and the Imam (a) did not only aim at providing people basic necessities, but he also provided them non-essential and luxury needs.

---

[61] A thorough study revealed that Arab youth yearn for change, but their economic dreams are hampered by narrow-minded societies that are not aware of their great potentials.

62 Refer to www.siironline.org.

Third: Cutting Back on Spending

The cutting back on spending that we clearly see in the government of Imam Ali (a) is considered to be one of the greatest foundations of a sound economy and putting an end to poverty. We have tens of examples that reflect how careful and exact Imam Ali (a) was in legislating laws that prevented wasting - even a single *dirham* (silver coin) from the people's wealth.

It is evident that if the general state of a society were to be very careful in spending, then the billions that are wasted on a daily basis would be saved. They might seem as a small drop in the bucket, but when collected, they form a huge budget which could then be spent on energizing the economy, the economic infrastructure, and to save the poor from their poverty.

Let us give several examples in this regards:

1. When a person came to see Imam Ali (a) to discuss with him a personal matter, the Imam (a) blew out the oil lamp (or candle) because it belonged to the Muslim treasury - in today's terms it was government money.
2. When writing letters, the Imam (a) would not leave any gaps between the lines (to save paper), and he passed a general law to his government employees that stated: "Sharpen your pens and keep your lines close to each other."[63]
3. Among the laws Imam Ali (a) passed in regards to writing letters was: "Omit anything that is unnecessary and get right to the point."[64] This law means that time is saved for the ruler and for the workers and employees. Time has great value, and all of that saved time represents a huge wealth for the country such that if it was to be spent in strategic, more important and fundamental matters, instead of being used for trivial issues and petty talk, then the country would advance and

[63] *Al-Khisaal*, p. 310.

[64] *Wasa'il al-Shia*, vol. 12, p. 299, ch. 15, hadith no. 2.

leap forward.

This was the state during the era of Imam Ali (a), in the third decade since the establishment of the Islamic government which coincided with the AD 7th century.

When we briefly examine how today, our Islamic countries are cutting back on spending, even though many of them have a rich economy and huge resources, we realize that there is a gap that exists between Imam Ali (a) cutting back on spending and these Islamic countries cutting back on spending.

When Imam Ali (a) instituted the policy of being economical and cutting back on spending, it was in the interest of the society and the Muslim society (the *ummah*); but the way that today's rulers are cutting back on spending is harming public interests. In essence, it is the people who are paying the price, not the government officials such as the president or minister, like it was during the time of Imam Ali (a).

Let us take a look at how our countries[65] cut back on spending today. In our countries, cutting back on spending is aimed at reducing services the government offers people in all sectors, such as healthcare, education, water and electricity, transportation, and telecommunications—all of which impose increased costs on individuals and families.

Furthermore, this subjects the country to economic and political pressures, as well as straining national security. This is caused by incorrect rationing, spending, or cutting back on spending because governments and political entities go on to expand their military and economic projects, and this has a drastic, negative impact on the economy. Examples include: making arms deals, multifaceted secret service programs, or unsuccessful investment projects given to foreign companies. All of this occurs at the expense of constricting lively matters.

What proves this point is that high-ranking government

---

[65] Even in democratic countries which, is evident for those who follow up with such matters.

employees oppose and reject any attempt to cut back on spending because it will cause them to concede many of their privileges and interests that they were accustomed to. This is what we observe in many Islamic countries. Therefore, if a government must cut back on spending, high-ranking government employees and officials do not want to be impacted by the spending cuts, so they will have the spending cuts applhy to the people only.

Fourth: Social Security[66]

Among the laws that Imam Ali (a) legislated with respect to social security is what he wrote in his treatise to Malik al-Ashtar:

> Fear Allah, fear Allah in (observing the rights of the) lower classes who cannot help themselves, such as the destitute, the needy, those who suffer from extreme poverty, and the disabled or chronically ill, for in this group there are those who ask and those who do not ask. Allah has assigned you to observe His right in them, so observe Allah's right (by observing the rights of those miserable people). Fix for them a share from the Muslim Treasury (public funds) and a share from the crops of lands taken over as booty for Islam in every city, and give them wherever they may be, whether close at hand or far away from you. All of these people are those whose rights have been placed in your charge. Therefore, a luxurious

[66] Today this is considered a public institution that has a social and administrative character to it. It enjoys a moral personality, financial independence, and joining it or being associated with it is compulsory. As for its services, it offers services to all working individuals and their families. The social insurances include sickness, birth, disability, work injuries or accidents, work-related illnesses, and unemployment by offering monetary or other types of support. As for its earnings or proceeds, they are achieved by subscriptions paid by business owners, employees, and social services funds. Social security is considered an institution (for compulsory reservation or storing).

> life should not keep you away from them.[67]

The social security or welfare system of Imam Ali (a) included the following:

1. Religious minorities. For example, the Imam (a) fixed a salary from public funds for the old Christian man who no longer had the ability to work.[68]
2. Islam imposed a rule on the Muslim Treasury (public funds) that it was to pay the debt of anyone who is incapable of repaying one's debt. Will we find anything similar to that in today's world?
3. Islam also imposed on the Muslim Treasury the requirement to take care of the expenses of any woman whose husband is incapable of supporting her; any son whose father is incapable

---

[67] *Nahj al-Balagha*, p. 436. Letter 53 (Letter of Imam Ali (a) to Malik al-Ashtar)

[68] The Grand Ayatollah Sayed Sadeq al-Shirazi states in his book *al-Siyasah min Waqe' al-Islam*: "Look at the following story and contemplate its far reaching implications. Sheikh Hurr al-Amili (may Allah have mercy on him) states in his book *Wasa'il al-Shi'a* that once, Imam Ali (a) was walking in the streets of Kufa when he saw a man begging. The Imam (a) then directed his question to those people around him saying: 'What is this?' They said: 'He is a Christian man who has become old and is no longer able to work, and he has no money to live on, so he begs people for money.' The Imam (a) said with anger: 'You used him when he was young and now that he has grown old you have abandoned him?' Then the Imam (a) fixed a salary from public funds for this man so he can live on it until he dies. This demonstrates that poverty had no room in the Islamic Government, as the Imam (a) would be surprised when he saw a single poor person, and he would consider it as an unnatural and inappropriate phenomenon or occurrence in an Islamic society and in an Islamic economy. Even though the man was a Christian who did not believe in Islam, the Imam (a) fixed a salary for him to subsist on. The Imam (a) did not want to have a single indication of poverty and hunger in an Islamic state. He also wanted the world and Muslims to know that an Islamic government eradicates poverty and improves living standards."

of supporting him; and any father whose son is incapable of supporting him.

In our modern times, welfare systems only include those who live in countries rich in oil, natural gas, or countries which have a strong economy. In addition to that, the current welfare systems are incomplete and twisted. As for poor countries, people lack basic needs for their everyday lives, let alone having a system that secures their futures.

Even the welfare system that exists in some of our countries today is a loose system that is not capable of facing economic and political challenges, and it does not extend coverage to all members of the society. It only covers those who are employed by the government.

As for the vast majority of people, such as businessmen, students, the elderly, and widows, they are left uninsured and their basic needs are not taken care of. In fact, insurance or welfare companies, in many instances, have become business corporations which are only concerned about making profits.

Fifth: Creating a Balance between Rural and Urban Areas

One of the most important factors that create economic instability (or imbalance) and help spread poverty is the emphasis of governments on urban areas at the expense of rural areas. This causes skilled and qualified works to migrate from rural areas to urban areas, since there will be more work opportunities in the cities, more economic comfort, and more incentives for them to migrate. In turn, this weakens agricultural output and increases poverty in rural areas. Rural areas will also suffer from a regression in education and this will naturally impact the economy.

Imam Ali (a) was the first person to call on the creation of a balance between the rural and urban areas, as he writes in his treatise to Malik al-Ashtar:

> And give them wherever they may be, whether close at hand (in the city) or far away from you (in rural areas); and all of these people are those whose rights have been placed in your charge.[69]

This excerpt means that the economic rights that people who live far away from the urban centers have—the residents of rural areas and villages—are identical to the economic rights the close ones have—the residents of the cities and urban areas.

As Imam Ali (a) says:

> And all of these people are those whose rights have been placed in your charge."

A ruler is responsible to observe both of these rights, and one is not allowed to neglect or abuse any of them.

The Imam (a) also says:

> Look after the revenue (*kharaj* or land tax) affairs in such a way that those engaged in it remain prosperous because in their prosperity lies the prosperity of all others.[70]

Thus, taking care of rural areas is a key factor in maintaining a healthy and progressive economy.

Sixth: Social Solidarity[71]

[69] *Nahj al-Balagha*, p. 438.

[70] Ibid., p. 436.

[71] Social solidarity means that members of a society take part in protecting public and private interests. They collaborate to deter any material or spiritual harms. Each member of a society feels that one has obligations towards other people just as one also has rights themselves. One also feels that they have a responsibility towards those who cannot fulfill their personal needs by offering them benefits and protecting them from harm.

Social solidarity in Islam is achieved in any society which implements the religion of Islam in its belief system, its *Sharia* (law), its code of conduct, and its way of life according to the Holy Quran and the *sunnah* (Prophet Muhammad's (s) way of life), and also according to Imam Ali's (a) way of life and method of governance.

Imam Ali (a) solidified the pillars of social solidarity, as Islam had laid the foundations for social solidarity in various dimensions. Social solidarity became one of the leading factors in combating poverty in addition to creating social stability.

1. Prophet Muhammad (s) said: "A person who sleeps with a full stomach while one's neighbor is hungry has not believed in me."[72]
2. He also said: "A person who sleeps having satisfied one's hunger and thirst, while one's neighbor is hungry and thirsty is not a believer."[73]

Imam al-Shirazi (may Allah have mercy on him) says in his book *al-Fiqh: al-Iqtisad*,[74] which is volume 107 of his encyclopedia named *al-Fiqh* on pages 298-299:

> This *hadith* (which says one is not a believer) is either a moral mandate which means that one has not achieved complete faith; or it is a legal mandate which means that those who are desperately in need are allowed to take what they need from those who have, such as during a famine. If one is desperate and in need during a famine, then one can take the necessary needs from someone (wealthy), and then one will have to compensate that person later. If a person is unable to compensate them later, then the state treasury must compensate for them.

Islam placed great emphasis on building a complete, inclusive society, and it brought forth a number of religious texts and laws aimed at actualizing the image which the Prophet (s) described by saying: "The likeness of believers in their compassion, mercy, and empathy, is like that of a singly body—if one of its organs suffers, then the entire body responds through fever and sleeplessness."

[72] *Al-Kafi*, vol. 2, p. 668.

[73] *Mustadrak al-Wasa'il*, vol. 8, p. 428.

[74] He has an encyclopedia on Islamic Law, and this particular volume is about the economy.

He also adds:

> If a person took what one needed as a loan, then one is required to pay it back within a year. If one is unable to repay it, then the state treasury must pay it.

Almighty Allah states in the Quran:

> Help one another in acts of righteousness and piety.[75]

Among the most apparent examples of "righteousness"[76] is the following verses:

> Or giving food on a day of hunger, to an orphan, near of kin, or to a destitute lying in the dust.[77]

1. Islam obligated a husband to take care of his wife's expenses.
2. It obligated a father to take care of his childrens' expenses as long as they are in need.
3. It obligated sons to take care of their parents' expenses as long as they are in need.

All of this amounts to restricting and confining poverty from every direction, as wives, parents and children constitute the majority of any given society.

All of this was implemented in the government of Imam Ali (a).[78]

---

[75] *Quran*, Surah al-Ma'idah (5), verse 2.

[76] Islam has placed an enormous amount of emphasis on empathy and sympathy in hundreds of verses and holy narrations. Refer to the book *Fiqh al-Ta'awon* (The Law of Collaboration) by the author.

[77] *Quran*, Surah al-Balad (90), verses 14-16.

[78] For further reading, refer to the book *Imam Ali (a): the Sun in the Horizon of Humanity* by the late Imam al-Shirazi; the book *al-Fiqh: al-Iqtisad* by Imam al-Shirazi; and also the book *al-Siyasah min Waqe' al-Islam* by the Grand Ayatollah Sayed Sadeq al-Shirazi.

Seventh: Creating Objective Standards for Economic or Financial Officers and Having them Observe those Standards

Imam Ali (a) established important and precise foundations and guidelines for all of those who manage the economy, such as the ruler or governor. This also included all of those who had the authority to make crucial decisions that affected the economic state of the people, such as the head of the central bank nowadays.

Among those guidelines are:

1. One must not be stingy, for a stingy person prefers to fill the reserves of the government and increase the percentage of all reserves,[79] even if one tries to justify that citing economic factors.[80] That person will even try to hinder any attempt aimed at delivering money to the people, will resist healthcare spending, will oppose increasing spending on education, and will even exert the effort to cut spending on all other humanitarian projects for the sake of increasing military expenditures. The United States of America serves as a suitable example, and many Islamic governments or regimes are also suitable examples of this.[81]

2. One must not lack any expertise; and therefore must have the highest levels of proficiency.

---

[79] This is the money or resources set aside for emergencies, or the money a government seeks when a need arises.

[80] The real reserves lies in the development of land, construction of factories, improving education, earning the trust of the people in the government, and so on. As for monetary reserves, only a small amount is required. In fact, if the government is a good and upright government, then the currency in the hands of the people will serve as a support to back the government without needing to store any money.

[81] Data released by the Congressional Research Service, which works for the US Congress, reveals that in 2010, Gulf countries spent more than $105 billion on armaments (or weapons purchases). This represented an increase of $11 billion over the previous year.

3. One should not be harsh or rough.
4. One should not be unfair to domestic or foreign groups, meaning that one should not favor this company or that organization, or a particular party or even a specific person.
5. A person should not be accepting of any bribery,[82] for it is obvious that the one who takes bribes will give special preference to the rich at the expense of the poor. For instance, instead of granting government contracts to the company or group which offers the best product for the least cost, one will offer those contracts to a group which gives him the most money or the most political backing, even though it is not the best group for that contract. This in turn deals a double blow to the economy and to the poor people.

Imam Ali (a) says:

> You certainly know that a person who is in charge of honor, life, booty, (enforcement of) legal commandments and the leadership of the Muslims should not be a miser, as one's greed will aim at their wealth; nor (should he) be ignorant, as he will then mislead them with his ignorance; nor be of rude behavior, as he would estrange them with his rudeness; nor should he deal unjustly with wealth by preferring one group over another; nor should he accept a bribe while making decision (in matters of governance).[83]

We have many narrations which point us to adopting fair and objective standards for rulers and officials, and the necessity of having them abide by those standards. Rulers should not exploit their political positions for economic or personal gains.

---

[82] Bribery is a type of corruption used to describe paying a person or an organization a sum of money or a service in return for benefiting from a right that one is not entitled to. Or it could be in return for being relieved from an obligation.

[83] *Nahj al-Balagha*, vol. 2, p. 14, sermon no. 131.

Here we shall mention a brief example of how Imam Ali (a) would exercise extreme caution to avoid using his political and governmental position to give special preference to the wealthy and the merchants.

It has been narrated that the Commander of the Faithful Imam Ali (a) visited *Dar Forat*, which was a fabric market, and he said (to one of the sellers):

> O man, make a good transaction with me by selling me a shirt for three *dirhams*.

When the seller recognized that it was Imam Ali (a), the Imam refused to buy from him. Then the Imam approached another seller, and when he also recognized him, he did not buy from him. Finally, the Imam approached a youth and bought a garment (or long shirt) from him for three *dirhams*. The Imam wore the garment, which covered him down to his ankles. Then the father of that boy came and he was told:

> Today your son sold the Commander of the Faithful (a) a shirt for three *dirhams*.

Then he told his son:

> Why did you not take from him two *dirhams* only?

His father took a *dirham* and went to see Imam Ali (a). The Imam was sitting at the *Rahba Gate* (in the Grand Mosque of Kufa) and the Muslims were gathered around him. The father said:

> Take this *dirham* O Commander of the Faithful.

The Imam replied:

> What is this for?

He said to him:

> The price of your shirt is two *dirhams*.

Imam Ali (a) replied to him:

> He sold it to me with my satisfaction and I took it with

> his satisfaction.[84]

Rulers and those with power should not exploit their positions, ranks, and influence in transactions, contracts, and especially in bids, as it is quite customary for those who have authority and power to bribe government officials so they get the bids or are awarded contracts.

Imam Ali (a) offered such a valuable lesson through this rare incident, and while it might seem simple and insignificant, he actually taught us an exemplary approach. If rulers adopt this approach, and if people pressure them to implement it, then the economic state of nations would change, and one of the primary causes of poverty would vanish.

Eighth: Establishing the Principles of Accountability and Answerability[85]

Imam Ali (a) established the principles of accountability, answerability and transparency. He also opened the door to dismiss any ruler who did not abide by the proper political and economic system which grants people their rights.

The Imam (a) says:

> Keep track of their activities and send truthful and trustworthy spies (or informants) to watch over them.[86]

This is among the most important differences between Islam and despotic regimes with respect to intelligence and monitoring. In Islam, based on the system created by Imam Ali (a), spies or informants monitor rulers, officials and those in charge of the economy, all for the interest of the people. The exact opposite is found in dictatorial regimes, where spies and informants are

---

[84] *Bihar al-Anwar*, vol. 40, p. 332, ch. 98, trad. 14. See also *Mustadrak al-Wasa'il*, vol. 13, p. 248.

[85] This factor is considered to be one of the most important factors in preserving or saving resources, as it also leads to the development of resources, even though it is not considered a factor in creating wealth.

[86] *Nahj al-Balagha*, vol. 2, p. 96.

planted to monitor the activities of the people for the interest of the rulers, governors and officials!

In this regards, let us read the full text of Imam Ali's (a) law as he lays it out in his letter to Malik al-Ashtar:

> You should also check their (the leaders) activities and have people who report on them who are truthful and faithful, because your watching their actions secretly will urge them to preserve trust and be kind to the people. Be careful of assistants. If any one of them extends his hands towards misappropriation, and the reports of your reporters reaching you confirms it, then that should be regarded enough evidence. You should then inflict corporal punishment on them and recover what they had misappropriated. You should put them in a place of disgrace, blacklist them with (the charge of) misappropriation, and make them wear the necklace of shame for their offence.

There is much to discuss about selections from this text, but we will defer that to another time.

Ninth: Stimulating the Flow of Money

The more there is a flow of capital, the more the economy becomes active and lively, as more money liquidity will circulate in the hands of the people. Transactions will become easier to conduct and inflation will go down. Hoarding[87] and stashing wealth, on the other hand, first of all freezes capital and prevents the flow of money; and secondly, it reduces or slows the capital or stock cycles. For this reason, Islam highly opposes piling up wealth. Allah states in the Holy Quran:

---

[87] Hoarding wealth means stockpiling currency or liquid money for a long period of time. The word '*kanz*' in Arabic (which the Quran in Surah al-Tawbah (9), verse 34 uses) literally means money or wealth that is buried in the ground. Hoarded money is kept stagnant and away from any circulation, without any direct benefits or economic gains.

> And as for those who amass gold and silver and do not spend them in the way of Allah, announce to them the tidings of a painful chastisement.[88]

The prohibition of hoarding wealth is not limited to gold and silver only, though they are among the clearest and most obvious examples of hoarding.

Governments today undertake this dangerous practice, which is stockpiling wealth, in the name of "government reserves." Billions or hundreds of billions are frozen this way, and this actually creates another more serious problem, which is having these huge sums of money in the hands of a bureaucratic management.[89]

To the contrary, we find that in the economic system of Imam Ali (a), money which is levied by taxes or other means was to be immediately distributed to the people. Hence, Imam Ali (a) would not allow any money to sit in the treasury even for a single night, and he would dispense that money the same day. At night, he would sweep the treasury room to indicate that no money remained in it.

This system results in having all of the money end up in the hands of the people, including the poor, thereby greatly minimizing the rates of poverty in society. Second, it speeds up the flow of capital in the economic wheel, in addition to its positive impact on the government and the people, as giving out all of the money to the people provides them with greater opportunities to develop the earth through construction, farming, pasturing or ranching, building factories, and making use of minerals and other resources. All of this translates into greater monetary returns for the people, which in turn also means greater returns

---

[88] *Quran*, Surah al-Tawbah (9) verse 34.

[89] Bureaucracy is a term used in sociology and political science that refers to the firm implementation of laws in organized societies. Such governments or systems rely on uniform procedures and the distribution of responsibilities in a hierarchical way and personal contacts or links.

for the government from taxes – which are levied justly – and once again that money goes back into the hands of the people.

Thus, we see that channeling foreign exchange reserves and gold into the hands of people provides an enormous potential in putting an end to poverty directly and indirectly. It also increases the credit and power of the government and the people because it greatly increases the gross domestic product (GDP). This is the real and active "reserves," and this is what serves as the bigger economic foundation which backs a country's currency.

Some researchers believe that the necessity of stimulating the flow of capital and speeding up its circulation was among the primary reasons behind the decision of Prophet Muhammad (s) to change the system of bartering goods to the monetary system and designating gold and silver as the standard.

The Prophet (s) also fixed the price of currency, as he fixed the price of a *dinar* as having a specific weight (called *mithqaal* in Arabic), and he fixed the price of a camel as being equivalent to one hundred *dinars*.[90]

It is quite evident that the monetary system[91] is better than the system of bartering goods, because the monetary system provides an easy medium to carry, transport, and circulate money. This medium is suited to be converted to any commodity or good, and vice-versa. It is also faster and more effective in the

---

[90] These details, however, require further research to ascertain their accuracy.

[91] Agreements were made at the Bretton Woods Conference to establish the new international monetary and financial order. It was necessary to have an international organization responsible for overseeing the implementation of the Bretton Woods agreement, as it also would be responsible to regulate financial and monetary transactions. It laid out a fixed system for regulating the price of currency exchange. This organization also had the right to monitor the performance of the new international monetary order. However, throughout time, some problems occurred with some underpinnings of this agreement causing the world to fall into other financial crises.

movement or transfer of wealth and eliminating inflation.

To the contrary, the system of bartering goods can leave goods either completely unused or unused for a time, and it can also lead to the decay or deterioration of many goods during the process of bartering and exchanging goods.

Tenth: Reducing Working Hours[92]

Islam called on reducing working hours both directly and indirectly, which means that the poor have greater room to participate in production and pull themselves out of poverty.

France has lately adopted this path. The National Institute of Statistics in France stated that reducing working hours from 39 hours per week to 35 hours provided 350,000 work opportunities from the time that this labor law was implemented in 1998; and until 2002, they had predicted that 600,000 work opportunities would be created. As for the rate of unemployment, it went down by 10% according to the Associated Press. Despite that, the French Parliament, which was controlled by conservatives, changed the law after that. The French labor law was inadequate (despite its relative success) because it did not offer a comprehensive solution to the problem (of poverty), meaning that it was attempting to solve only one aspect of the problem.[93]

Imam Ali (a) called for the reduction of working hours through various methods such as the following:

1. He encouraged leaving the markets early.
2. Being timely in performing the daily prayers, which meant leaving the market daily twice or more.
3. He encouraged people to set a decent amount of time for worship, family, friends, and recreation. One hadith states: "It

[92] Reducing the hours of working provides employment opportunities to millions of unemployed people. Therefore, we have considered it as one of the factors that create wealth for the deprived. It also reduces the pressure and stress from employees and workers.

[93] Source: Arabic CNN, accessed on 25/6/2006.

is incumbent on a rational person, if one is rational, to divide his day into four parts: one part praying to His Lord, one part holding himself accountable..."[94]

Eleventh: Being Flexible with Taxes

Unfair taxes are considered to be among the most important causes of poverty. We have explained in another section that imposing taxes on consumption instead of on profit is among the causes of poverty. The religion of Islam imposed dues on profits, such as *khums*,[95] *zakat*,[96] and land tax - but not on consumption, as is evident.

We propose that among the solutions–in addition to the importance of having taxes be imposed on profit, not consumption–is to have the tax system that is flexible and lenient. The tax rate should decrease whenever the rate of profits decreases. This is consistent with the intellect and power of reason. In this regard, we read the following in the text of Imam Ali's (a) humane law:

> If they (those from whom you take taxes) complain about heaviness,[97] or diseases,[98] or dearth of water,[99] or excess of water,[100] or a change in the condition of the land[101] either due to a flood or a drought, then you should decrease

[94] *Bihar al-Anwar*, vol. 1, p. 131. Also refer to *Rawdhah al-Wa'idhin*, p. 4.

[95] *Khums* is an obligation to pay one-fifth of one's unused profits for charitable causes.

[96] *Zakat* includes many types of charities, dues and tithes, but the most common type is to pay *zakat* on cattle and crops if one owns a certain amount of them.

[97] Such as disease inflicting their crops, or a disease which afflicts them and thus makes it heavy for them to produce sufficiently.

[98] Such as a natural misfortune (not human induced) afflicting their crops.

[99] The water used to irrigate the crops.

[100] The water which floods the area where the crops are grown.

[101] Such as the decomposition or rotting of the seeds.

> the taxes to the extent that there is a hope that it will improve their situation.

Since Imam Ali (a) knew very well that governments and rulers find it very difficult, or even quite impossible, to reduce taxes, he continued to say:

> You should not grudge or feel heavy for the reduction (of taxes) granted by you for the removal of distress, because it is an investment which they will return to you in the shape of the prosperity of your country and the progress of your domain, in addition to earning their praise and happiness for meeting out justice to them. You can depend upon their strength because of the investment made by you in them through catering to their convenience, and you can have confidence in them because of the justice extended to them by being kind to them. After that, circumstances may turn such that you have to ask for their assistance, and they will bear it happily, for prosperity is capable of hearing whatever you load on it. The ruin of a land is caused by the poverty of its cultivators, and the cultivators become poor when the officers concentrate on the collection (of money), having little hope for continuance (in their posts) and deriving no benefits from the objects of warning.[102]

Twelfth: Granting Freedoms

The general principle in Islam is freedom, for Almighty Allah has considered freedom as one of the foremost objectives behind the message of Prophet Muhammad (s). The Quran says:

> And removes from their burdens and the shackles that were upon them.[103]

Imam Ali (a) said:

---

[102] *Nahj al-Balagha*, letter 53, Imam Ali's (a) letter to Malik al-Ashtar.

[103] *Quran*, Surah al-A'raf (7) verse 157.

> O people, Adam did not beget any male or female slaves. All people are free.[104]

He also said:

> One of the successes of a free person is to make a lawful living.[105]

As well he has said that:

> There is no room for malice and deception in freedom.[106]

Finally a statement reads:

> Whoever frightens people has dissociated oneself from freedom.[107]

Therefore, freedom is the first factor leading to economic development and progress, and thus we see that the late Imam al-Shirazi issued a ruling prohibiting anything that reduces economic production.[108] He also said in his legal work entitled

---

[104] *Al-Kafi*, vol. 8, p. 69.

[105] *Ghurar al-Hikam*, p. 354.

[106] Ibid., p. 291.

[107] Ibid., p. 204.

[108] Refer to the Arabic book *Studies on the Thought of Imam al-Shirazi* available on the website for Imam Shirazi Center for Studies (www.siironline.org). He says: "Dumping the market means exporting services or goods to a market in another country at a price below the cost of production, or the price charged in that importing country. Dumping the market can lead to laying off workers and employees, the shutting down of factories or their bankruptcy, a decrease in production, and major economic, social and political disturbances. Thus, dumping the market is considered unfair competition and it is unjust. That is why it faces opposition from the importing country and its companies."

The late Imam al-Shirazi, may Allah have mercy on him, also said in his book *Fiqh al-Muroor*, pages 176-177 that: "Doing business is free except for prohibited businesses or doing business with harmful substances such as drugs. In Islamic lands there is no such thing as trafficking or smuggling. Yes, the law of "no harm" must be upheld, so a businessman must not import or export that which inflicts harm

Globalization:

> Any law or proposal which causes a reduction in production, whether in agriculture or manufacturing, is prohibited. It is also prohibited to plan and execute anything which harms the human being and scars his honor or dignity, even if it is by decreasing his daily income.[109]

Freedom is also the foremost factor in exploding potentials and in the development of talents and innovations, which means a greater opportunity for inventions and discoveries, and greater room for technological pursuits, both in agriculture and manufacturing. Consequently, there will be a greater opportunity to combat poverty quickly and effectively.

For further reading on this topic, one may refer to the books *al-Fiqh al-Hurriyaat* (The Jurisprudence of Freedoms), *al-Fiqh al-Iqtisaad* (The Jurisprudence of Economy), and *al-Siyaghah al-Jadidah* by the late Imam al-Shirazi. In these books, the late author demonstrates that the economic freedoms in our world today do not even reach 10% of the economic freedoms granted by Islam.[110]

---

on Muslims or non-Muslims living in Islamic lands. One also has no right to import that which may inflict harm on Muslims such as causing them to be laid off or become unemployed. A person also has no right to export that which inflicts harm on Muslims or non-Muslims, such as causing a harmful rise in prices. As for customs taxes, they are definitely prohibited, and it is a form of usurping the possessions of people by false means, regardless of what it is called, and therefore taking such taxes makes one liable to pay them back to the people. If a person knowingly or deliberately takes such prohibited taxes, then one deserves punishment according to the Islamic law."

[109] *Al-Fiqh al-Awlama* (*The Jurisprudence of Globalization*), by Imam al-Shirazi, p. 216.

[110] The late Grand Ayatollah Imam Sayed Mohammad al-Shirazi states: "Freedom in Islam is a right before anything else. The one who researches this matter will realize that Islam has granted 100%

freedoms, whereas the freedoms granted today in the world which is called "the free world" is only 10% of that or even less.

Islam granted the human being the freedom of thought, the freedom of speech, and the freedom of work - but within an appropriate and rational framework, such as not harming others, nor significantly harming oneself. For instance, drinking and eating that which may inflict major harm on oneself are prohibited, and slandering and hitting are also prohibited because they inflict harm on others. In addition, using resources more than what is reasonable and appropriate is also prohibited because it harms future generations.

Freedom then, includes all people - even the non-believers in all fields and areas. Some examples include intellectual freedom, meaning the freedom to research, debate and discuss scientific and religious issues. Among the freedoms is economic freedom, meaning the freedom to make a living and do business. Religious freedom, meaning being tolerant of other religions. Political freedom which concerns the relationship between the ruler and the ruled. The ruler must be elected by the people and must meet the criteria that satisfy Allah the Almighty and other Islamic criteria, all of which are rational criteria. For instance, a ruler must be knowledgeable (about ruling and governance), mature, just, and possess other qualities which scholars have discussed in the chapter on *Taqlid* (emulation).

We have mentioned a number of *ahadith* about choosing a ruler in our book, *al-Hukm fi al-Islam* (Governance in Islam) and in our other Islamic books. There are one hundred examples for Islamic freedom, and we shall refer to them here. They include:

1. The freedom to worship in any place, whether it is praying, fasting, performing ablution, remembering Allah, reading the Quran, or supplicating to Allah. As for prayer, it possess absolute freedom, for the Prophet (s) has said: "The earth has been made for me a place for prostration and a place of purity."

2. The freedom to buy.

3. The freedom to sell.

4. The freedom to lease.

5. The freedom to guarantee.

6. The freedom to innovate any new contract which Islam has not prohibited.

7. The freedom to pledge security as a guarantee (*kafalah*).
8. The freedom to reconcile.
9. The freedom to provide insurance.
10. The freedom to make a partnership.
11. The freedom to make a joint business venture called "*mudharabah*."
12. The freedom to sharecropping.
13. The freedom to irrigate crops and be paid for that.
14. The freedom to develop unowned land.
15. The freedom to own unowned resources.
16. The freedom to consignment.
17. The freedom to loan.
18. The freedom to rent.
19. The freedom to power of attorney.
20. The freedom to make an endowment.
21. The freedom to give charity.
22. The freedom to donate.
23. The freedom to gift.
24. The freedom to reside.
25. The freedom to construct.
26. The freedom to racing.
27. The freedom to archery.
28. The freedom to make a will.
29. The freedom to marry, for both men and women, whether in a permanent or temporary marriage.
30. The freedom to divorce.
31. The freedom to make a *khul'a* divorce.
32. The freedom to breastfeed.
33. The freedom to travel.
34. The freedom to stay home.

35. The freedom to open a store.

36. The freedom to admit or confess.

37. The freedom to offer a reward for something.

38. The freedom to print.

39. The freedom to designate the amount of dowry and other details concerning marriage.

40. The freedom to seek any profession one desires.

41. The freedom to education, meaning to seek knowledge that benefits oneself, others, animals, plants, or other things. Hence, one may become a physician, engineer, lawyer, political expert, economic expert, religious jurist, speaker or author.

42. The freedom to make a religiously binding promise.

43. The freedom to make an oath.

44. The freedom to a religious vow.

45. The freedom to eat lawful foods in any way one desires.

46. The freedom to develop dead lands.

47. The freedom to buy the share of one's partner if they sell their share to a third person without permission.

48. The freedom to inheritance, so the inheritors are entitled to the amounts designated by the Prophet (s) according to Islamic law. The Prophet (s) said: "Whoever leaves behind a family which has no sponsor or leaves behind a loan, then I will take care of them, and whoever leaves behind wealth, it is for the inheritors." Current man-made laws however, sometimes stipulate that as high as 90% of the inheritance is to be given to the government.

49. The freedom to refer to any legitimate judge.

50. The freedom to witness or seek witnesses.

51. The freedom to choose the blood money, to choose retribution or to pardon in certain cases.

52. The freedom to farm.

53. The freedom to manufacture.

54. The freedom to build.

55. The freedom to be without citizenship.

56. The freedom to issue a newspaper.

57. The freedom to issue a magazine.

58. The freedom to own a broadcasting station.

59. The freedom to own a television broadcasting station.

60. The freedom to work.

61. The freedom to express one's opinions.

62. The freedom to assembly.

63. The freedom to form unions.

64. The freedom to establish associations.

65. The freedom to make organizations.

66. The freedom to form parties.

67. The freedom to elect.

68. The freedom to rule.

69. The freedom to govern.

70. The freedom to be an ambassador.

71. The freedom to choose any government job.

72. The freedom to privacy, meaning that a government should not spy on people through communication devices, telephones, or other means used by intelligence agencies.

73. The freedom to bear any number of children.

74. The freedom to marry up to four permanent wives and more temporary wives.

75. The freedom to believe, as Allah states: "There is no compulsion in religion."

76. The freedom to eat, drink and wear what one wants.

77. The freedom to leave the house and return back anytime one desires, whether at night or during the day. In some cities like Moscow or other communist cities, people do not have the freedom to travel except to a specific extent. Similarly, people do not have freedom when there is a curfew in other cities.

---

78. The freedom to build mosques.

79. The freedom to build schools.

80. The freedom to build *Husayniyyas.*

81. The freedom to build hospitals.

82. The freedom to build clinics.

83. The freedom to establish publishing companies.

84. The freedom to build educational centers.

85. The freedom to build hotels and motels.

86. The freedom to build birthing centers.

87. The freedom to build hospices or nursing homes.

88. The freedom to open banks.

89. The freedom to join student unions.

90. The freedom to exit any institution or job, unless a person made a binding commitment not to leave.

91. The freedom to choose the type of furniture for one's store, office or house.

92. The freedom to choose any type of car one desires.

93. The freedom to make any type of transaction.

94. The freedom to seek a loan or give a loan.

95. The freedom to authorize whomsoever one wants to manage an endowment.

96. The freedom to name any person or place without needing a permit or authorization from the government.

97. The freedom to open poultry farms.

98. The freedom to emulate any qualified Grand Ayatollah.

99. The freedom to choose any speaker one wants.

100. The freedom to make a marriage contract under any scholar one chooses, without needing to register in government register offices. There are many other freedoms which Islam has granted. Refer to the book *al-Siyaghah al-Jadidadh* available at www.siironline.org.

Thirteenth: The Role of a Government is Supervision and Planning, not Production

It is incumbent on the government to assume excellent responsibility of supervision and organizing the country's affairs, establishing justice, and planning to uplift the economy. At the same time, it should abstain from assuming any economic role which takes the role of people, whether companies or individuals. Therefore: "nationalization,"[111] which restricts national resources in the hands of the government, is a grave mistake. The direct involvement of the government in production is also another mistake.

It is important to note than the idea of "nationalization" emerged as a means to save nations from past colonial powers who controlled their natural resources and agricultural wealth, especially oil. However, this turned out to be a curse on the nations instead of a blessing, since the ownership of all resources should be for the people. As for very big resources which individuals cannot manage, then a group representing the people and elected by the people should manage them, not the government.[112]

All of this will lead to the spread of poverty, and Imam Ali (a) says to Malik al-Ashtar in his letter to him:

> Now take some advice about traders and industrialists.

---

[111] Nationalization is to transfer the ownership of certain sectors to the government, meaning to make it public sector. This is a process which an "independent government" usually goes through within the frame of transferring ownership and solidifying the pillars of sovereignty such that the government assumes ownership of what it wants to nationalize. It is also an ongoing process which gives ownership of natural resources such as forests and minerals to the government.

[112] For details, see the book, *The Features of the Relation between the State and the People*, in Arabic, by the author. Also see the book, *The Jurisprudence of Rights*, the book, *The Jurisprudence of the Islamic Government*, and the book, *The Jurisprudence of the Economy* by the late Imam al-Shirazi.

> Give them good counsel...Look after their affairs before yourself or wherever they may be in your area...

The Imam (a) also said:

> Look after the revenue (*kharaj* - land tax) affairs in such a way that those engaged in it remain prosperous...[113]

The responsibility of a ruler is to supervise, provide economic security, make sure the process of production is safe and sound, not to be directly involved in the production of goods or in the services. This discussion is quite long and has many points, and it is possible to do further reading on it by referring to *The Jurisprudence of Politics*, *The Jurisprudence of the Economy*, and *The Jurisprudence of the Islamic Government*, all authored by the late Imam Shirazi, may Allah have mercy on him.

Another important point here is that it is incumbent on governors, rulers, ministers, and other government officials to work. First, this will relieve a big burden from the state's budget; and second, government officials will come to know the value of working more. This will push them to exert serious efforts in improving work opportunities and work conditions for the people. Consequently, the people will come to like their rulers more and support them more, thereby making their countries more stable and more secure. Third, all of this will serve to improve production opportunities and economic output.

We have many *ahadith* urging rulers and government officials to work, and history also tells us about some righteous governors who worked. We will present a few brief examples here.

Governors Should Also Work

History has recorded that Salman, who was the governor of Mada'in (a city in Iraq), would weave the leaves of palm trees, then he would sell them and make a living. He would say:

> I do not want to eat except from the work of my own

---

[113] *Nahj al-Balagha*, p. 436, letter 53.

hands.

He learned how to weave palm tree leaves when he was in Medina.[114]

All rulers, governors, ministers and government officials should work, and if all of them work and make a living, then they would not burden the state's treasury so much.

In some countries, the state treasury has to bear the burden of millions or hundreds of millions for the salary of government officials. Consider how much money could be saved for the poor.

Weave Palm Tree Leaves and Do Not Steal the Money of Others

In a letter from Salman, the servant of Prophet Muhammad (s), to Umar ibn al-Khattab reads:

> As for what you have mentioned, that I weave palm tree leaves and eat barley, then know that these two are not grounds for shaming a believer and rebuking him. I swear by Allah, O Umar, that weaving palm tree leaves and eating barley instead of eating expensive food and drinking expensive drinks, and instead of stealing the rights of a believer and making claims to what one has no right to, is better and more beloved to Almighty Allah and is closer to piety. Indeed, I saw the Messenger of Allah (s), when he had some barely, he would eat from it, and be satisfied, and he would not be irritated.[115]

Here we have some important realities to reflect upon:

1. Working is an honor - even if it appears humble or low, in the eyes of people.
2. Those who feel too high or proud to work by arguing that it is lowly or abject, usually fall into the pitfalls of making

---

[114] *Mustadrak al-Wasa'il*, vol. 13, p. 60, ch. 26, trad. 1.

[115] *Al-Ihtijaj*, vol. 1, pp. 130-131. Also refer to *Jame' Ahadith al-Shia*, vol. 17, p. 134.

unlawful profits. Such people try to find the easiest means to become wealthy, so they fall into deception and fraud, stealing and embezzlement, or monopolization and raising prices. Therefore, Salman said: "...weaving palm tree leaves and eating barley instead of eating expensive food and drinking expensive drinks, and instead of stealing the rights of a believer and making claims to what one has no right to, is better and more beloved to Almighty Allah and is closer to piety..."

3. A believer should be satisfied with what is available even if it seems meager. In fact, one should be happy with it just like Prophet Muhammad (s), as it is narrated that: "When he would have some barely, he would eat from it, and be satisfied, and he would not be irritated." Being satisfied with what is available and even being happy about it positively impacts one's physical and psychological wellbeing, and it also lowers stress. That in turn, positively impacts production, the ability to work more efficiently, and also one's family conditions.

Fourteenth: Combating

All Other Causes of Wasting Resources and Destroying the Economy

God-Willing, we will assign the third chapter to discuss this factor.

Section Two

Religious and Moral Factors for the Creation, Conservation and Development of Wealth and Combating Poverty

What we mean by religious factors are things such as piety and the avoidance of usury or interest. Religious factors bring about Divine blessings in unseen ways, and they also bring about the mercy of Allah in granting sustenance to His servants from His unseen treasuries when He finds them obedient to His commands. Allah says:

> There is nothing except that its treasures are with Us, and We do not send it down except in a known measure.[116]

Allah also says in the Quran:

> Had the people of those towns believed and been pious, We would have certainly opened up to them the blessings from the heavens and the earth. But they gave the lie (to their prophets) and so We seized them for their deeds.[117]

As for moral or ethical factors, such as being truthful, honest and fair, they are a series of moral factors, but they indirectly lead to the production and conservation of wealth. If people know that a businessman or retailer is honest, truthful and fair, then they will trust him, go to him, and so his clients will increase. People will keep their money with him, open up their hearts to him, help him in his business endeavors, and they will also assist him with their business relations.

This serves to demonstrate that religious and moral factors will essentially create wealth, conserve wealth and develop it. These factors are similar to those discussed in the first chapter, but a separate chapter has been set for these factors because the factors discussed in the first chapter are generally material or natural ones based on tangible economic equations.

As for the factors discussed in the second chapter, however, they are unseen and intangible factors, and from a material perspective, they are not generally known by most people or by material-based people for their impact on the economy. Thus, we designated a separate chapter for them to highlight their significance and importance.

---

[116] *Quran*, Surah al-Hijr (15) verse 21.

[117] *Quran*, Surah al-A'raf (7) verse 96.

Religious/Moral Recommendations which Have Significant Economic Outcomes

The following will be a series of religious and moral solutions for the problem of poverty, the proliferation of wealth, the conservation of wealth, and the development of it.

Imam Ali (a) has mentioned these solutions in his wills and advice to others, and we will discuss them in brief.

If people were to implement the general recommendations of this Imam, those which we have discussed and will discuss, then poverty would be totally uprooted. His recommendations were moral and divine, but they have significant social and economic outcomes.

Here are some of those recommendations:

Be God-Conscious or Pious

In one of his sayings, Imam Ali (a) says:

> O community of merchants, be God-conscious.[118]

It is evident that the awareness of God restrains people from sucking the blood of the poor through deception, fraud, cheating, monopolization, and raising prices. Piety serves to decrease poverty in all areas.

Start with "Istekhara"

In Arabic, the word "*istekhara*" means asking for God's blessings, as it is recommended for a servant of God, before doing a task, to ask the Lord to bless one's endeavor and what one plans to undertake. Among the ways to invoke God's blessings is to say:

> I ask for Allah's blessings with His mercy, and I ask Him to make that blessing in good health and welfare.

It is also best to pray two *rak'as* (units of prayer).

Since Allah is the Giver of sustenance, the Lord of all Power

---

[118] *Al-Kafi*, vol. 5, p. 151.

and the Strong, then He will bless any action or endeavor for which a person asks "*istekhara.*"

Take Ease or Lenience as a Way

Imam Ali (a) says:

> And see the blessings through ease.[119]

In another narration, the Imam (a) says:

> Make your transactions simple and easy.

Any administrative routine, complication or bureaucracy will hinder the flow of capital, increase costs, consume a great amount of time, enlarge the administrative apparatus, increase the number of employees, and place immense pressure on one's health and nervous system. This, consequently, creates illnesses which inflict stress on the poor.

Therefore, any sale or contract should be conducted with the utmost ease, free from any hard routine and complications.

We find that some governments in the world today started to adopt the approach of minimizing administrative routines in registering companies and in all other transactions. In Islam, there is no need for any of that!

Get Close to Clients[120]

Imam Ali (a) says:

> Get close to the buyers and sellers.[121]

The presence of many intermediaries or brokers causes rising prices and inflation because intermediaries or brokers live on raising the price ceiling so that they can make a profit. Sometimes they even make manifold profit. Hence, the more such intermediaries are eliminated, the lower prices will become

---

[119] Ibid.,

[120] Clients are those who make business deals with you; so try to eliminate intermediaries or brokers.

[121] *Al-Kafi*, vol. 5, p. 151.

and the lower the rate of poverty will be.

The government must come up with a plan to eliminate intermediaries because they increase the likelihood of manipulating the market given the great power that such companies—which act as intermediaries or brokers—enjoy.

Adorn Yourselves with Tolerance

Tolerance is the key to the hearts, and it is the best means to build bridges of love with others. For this reason, people flock to work with tolerant people and collaborate with them. If you want the Lord to open for you the doors of sustenance, then be tolerant and forbearing with employees, workers and partners.

Also be tolerant with and kind business or company owners, clients, and all of those to whom you sell and buy them from. Furthermore, be tolerant and forbearing with your family, children and relatives, and even with your enemies.

According to one narration:

> Tolerance adorns everything it is placed on, and intolerance strips everything (makes it ugly) that it is placed on.

Another tradition states:

> It is as if the tolerant, forbearing one is almost a prophet.

Avoid Making Oaths

According to a narration attributed to the Imam (a), he said:

> Beware of swearing by Allah, for it makes goods perish and deprives the blessings.[122]

We have explained the reason behind that in another part of this book.

Be Truthful

Imam Ali (a) says:

---

[122] Ibid., vol. 5, p. 162, trad. 4. Also refer to *Wasa'il al-Shia*, vol. 17, p. 419.

Avoid lying.[123]

Dishonesty in transactions results in greater pressure on the poor. Businessmen or companies lie to sell their products for a higher price, or they sell low quality products by advertising them to be high quality.

Avoid Oppression

The evil and prohibition of oppression are rationally self-evident.[124] In fact, it is recognized by the *fitrah*, or primordial human nature. Furthermore, oppression invites further oppression, and just like you treat others, you will be treated.

Therefore, a merchant should beware of his not being fair with his clients or cheating them, whether the oppression is conspicuous or discreet. Otherwise, Allah will empower someone to oppress him, and then he will find no one to aid him against his oppressor. As the poet says:

Do not oppress when you have the power to do so, for oppression brings about regret in the end.

Your two eyes sleep but the oppressed is awake, praying against you, and the eyes of God never sleep.

One tradition states that the Almighty Allah has said:

> ...does not oppress and no oppression can escape Him, for He is ever watchful. He will requite the evil-doers for their deeds and bestow a good reward on those who have done good. Whoever does good, does so to his own benefit, and whoever does evil, will suffer its evil consequences. Your Lord does no wrong to His servants.[125]

[123] *Al-Kafi*, vol. 5, p. 151.

[124] Meaning that the intellect recognizes that oppression is bad and disgraceful without needing the aid of religious texts.

[125] *Bihar al-Anwar*, vol. 73, p. 373, ch. 67.

Defend the Oppressed

Imam Ali (a) says:

> And defend the oppressed.[126]

In his letter to Malik al-Ashtar, he says:

> Fear Allah and keep Allah in view in respect to the lowest class, consisting of those who have few means: the poor, the destitute, the penniless and the disabled.

In any transaction, it is mandatory to be fair with the oppressed before having them go and file a complaint against the oppressor. If an oppressed party, whether it be an individual, a company or group, files a complaint against an oppressor, then the oppressor must immediately retract his unjust act. If he does not do so, then in addition to it being a violation of human rights, it will serve to add further pressure on the poor because lawyers will become wealthy at the expense of both parties.[127]

Furthermore, the oppressor or the oppressed (depending on who loses the case) will try to compensate for the money that was spent on lawyers and litigation by raising prices, or by deciding against giving employees a raise, all of which means more pressure on the poor.

---

[126] *Al-Kafi*, vol. 5, p. 151.

[127] Edward McCracken, who was the CEO of Silicon Graphics says: "I believe that almost all Silicon Valley companies filed numerous lawsuits against it, such as Hewlett Packard, Intel and our company. In reality, when a company is sued and a big settlement is reached, stock holders do not benefit as individuals. Instead, Bill Lerach (a famous lawyer) and his friends are the ones to benefit and make a lot of money this way." Source: the Arabic translation of the book, *In the Company of Giants* by Jager and Ortiz, p. 317.

Avoid Usury/Interest

Imam Ali (a) says:

> Do not come near usury.[128]

He also says in *Nahj al-Balagha*, quoting Prophet Muhammad (s):

> O Ali, people will fall into mischief through their wealth ... they will then hold lawful (the use of) alcohol by calling it barley water, a bribe by calling it a gift, and taking interest by calling it sale.[129]

The reason why we consider interest a religious or unseen factor even though it is an economic factor since it makes the rich richer, is that while interest is a material factor, not taking interest is a religious/unseen factor that increases wealth. If a person avoids dealing with interest, then the Almighty Allah will bless his wealth and open for him unexpected prospects for increasing his wealth or protecting it, or Allah might protect him from imminent dangers, such as a car accident.

If one was to deal with interest however then that calamity may have struck him, stripping him from his health and wealth, as he would have to spend it on seeking treatment or protecting himself from that misfortune to no avail. We have discussed this in another part of the book.

Upholding Honesty

The Almighty Allah says:

> Give full measure and weight with justice, do not diminish the goods of others, and do not go about creating corruption in the land.[130]

In addition, Imam Ali (a) says:

---

[128] *Al-Kafi*, vol. 5, p. 151.

[129] *Nahj al-Balagha*, sermon 156.

[130] *Quran*, Surah Hud (11) verse 85.

> Let the sale be a fair and easy sale, conducted with fair balances and prices which are not unfair to both parties, the buyer and the seller.[131]

This means that it is prohibited to manipulate the market, as we have mentioned before.

Do Business with God through Charity

Imam Ali (a), says:

> If abject poverty strikes you, then do business with Allah through charity.[132]

Charity has a direct impact on containing poverty, as it is evident. It also has an indirect impact, even though it is a fundamental and strategic impact.

Charity strengthens social solidarity and increases the bonds of love among community members, all of which reflect positively on production. This is in addition to the religious or divine factor, as sustenance is in the hands of Allah, for He says:

> Surely Allah is the Giver of sustenance, the Lord of all power, the Strong.[133]

Imam Ali (a) says:

> Richness and poverty will follow presentation before Allah.[134]

When Allah sees His servant donating despite onself being in need, then He will open for him a door to sustenance from where he imagines, and He may also give him sustenance from where

---

[131] *Nahj al-Balagha*, Imam Ali's letter to Malik al-Ashtar.

[132] *Nahj al-Balagha*, maxim 258.

[133] *Quran*, Surah al-Dhariyat (51), verse 58.

[134] *Nahj al-Balagha*, maxim 452. This means that a rich person is not really considered rich unless he achieves Divine reward in the Hereafter, and a poor person is not really considered poor unless he misses out on Divine reward, which makes him eternally miserable.

he never even imagined.

This factor does not apply to individuals only, as it also applies to companies and governments. Furthermore, if giving charity becomes commonplace and widespread, then the person himself will benefit when circumstances change and become the opposite. For instance, today this person gives charity to that person, but later the days will spin and that person may give charity to this person. Hence, charity is a fundamental, significant and comprehensive type of social security and solidarity.

Keep Ties with your Kin

Keeping ties with one's kin is among the significant religious/divine and natural factors in putting an end to poverty. Imam Ali (a) says:

> Behold! If any one of you finds your near ones in want or starvation, then do not desist from helping them with that which will not increase him[135] if this help is not extended, nor decrease him by thus spending it.[136]

Then the Imam (a) explains the benefit of helping one's kin by alerting us that our kin are:

1. The most concerned about us and the most supporting of us behind our back.
2. The best who can ward off our troubles.
3. They are the most compassionate to us when tribulations befall us.

---

[135] This means that if one keeps that money for oneself and does not give it to one's needy relatives, it will not really increase the sustenance which God has determined for them. For example, instead of benefitting from that money which he withheld from giving to his needy relatives, God will test him and he will end up having to spend it on treating an illness which would not have befallen him had he given that money to his kin.

[136] *Nahj al-Balagha*, sermon 23.

4. The good memory of a person that Allah retains among people[137] is better than the money which one bequeaths to others as inheritance."[138]

Therefore, keeping ties with one's kin has a direct impact, emotionally and materialistically, on curbing poverty areas, as is evident. It also creates a social foundation for eliminating poverty because keeping ties with one's kin makes the hearts close to each other and brings the hands together so that through collaboration, people become more capable in collectively combating poverty and continually uplifting the economy.

This is why we find that many family businesses are successful as long as they keep ties with one another; and whenever disputes grapple them, and they cut ties with each other, and the bonds of love and compassion are broken, then they fail.

Keeping ties with one's kin is considered as one of the most important factors in keeping people stress free and in eliminating depression. It is also a factor which increases self-confidence. All of this reflects positively on a person's ability to uplift the economy.

To the contrary, severing ties with one's kin is among the greatest factors in causing depression, destroying one's health, and being responsible for a number of diseases and conditions. Consequently, this weakens a person's ability to undertake sound economic planning, exceptional management, and good performance. It also shortens one's life, and thus Imam Ali (a) said:

> O Nawf, keep ties with your kin, and Allah will prolong your life.[139]

Imam al-Ridha (a) has said:

---

[137] Such good memory is attained by being truthful and honest with people.

[138] *Nahj al-Balagha*, sermon 23.

[139] *Bihar al-Anwar*, vol. 4, p. 89.

> Keeping ties with one's kin improves one's attitude and morals, makes one's hand more generous, makes one's self good and pure, increases one's sustenance, and prolongs one's life.[140]

In another narration, Imam Ali (a) said:

> Calamities befall when family ties are severed.[141]

In a final narration, he said:

> If people sever their family ties, money will end up in the hands of the evil ones.[142]

Severing family ties is among the leading factors which destroy the family and cause the children to be lost, which means:

1. The wealth that a family owned will be transferred through inheritance or other means, to corrupt or crooked children (as a result of their broken families).
2. The wealth of a family, due to it being broken and corrupted, will be wasted on unlawful acts, such as gambling, drinking, or illicit sexual relationships, all of which means that this wealth will end up in the hands of corrupt people.
3. The wealth of righteous families who broke their family ties will end up in the hands of unrighteous and corrupt families who maintained their family ties because those righteous families will go bankrupt due to their disputes and severing of ties, while the corrupt families will hold each other's backs.[143]

For these and other reasons, Imam al-Baqir (a) says:

---

[140] *Al-Kafi*, vol. 2, p. 151.

[141] *Ghurar al-Hikam*, p. 406.

[142] *Bihar al-Anwar*, vol. 74, p. 138.

[143] With respect to charity, keeping family ties and other righteous acts, refer to the book *al-Fiqh: al-Adab wa al-Sunan*; and the chapter on "*ishra*," or family and social relations, in the books of *Bihar al-Anwar*, *Wasa'il al-Shia*, and *al-Kafi*.

> Keeping ties with one's kin builds homes and prolongs lives even if the members of these families are not righteous.[144]

Let the Keys to the Realm of the Unseen Help You

It has been narrated that the Commander of the Faithful Imam Ali (a) said:

> If making a living becomes impossible for you and the doors to earning money are closed on you, then write the following prayer on piece of deer skin[145] or any other piece of skin, and carry it with you (like a necklace) or keep it in the clothes you wear. If you do this, then Allah will expand your sustenance and open paths for you to make a living from where you never even imagined. Write: 'O my dear Lord! So and so person, son/daughter of so and so person[146] has no power to strive, has no patience in the face of difficulty, and cannot bear being poor and needy. O my dear Lord, send your prayers on Muhammad and the family of Muhammad, and do not deny so and so person, son/daughter of so and so person, of your sustenance, and do not give him very little of the vastness of what You own, and do not deprive him of your favor, and do not reduce his share from the abundance of what You give, and do not submit his affairs to Your creation,[147] or his own self because he will be incapable of helping himself and is too weak to take it upon himself to do what is suitable for him and to also fix the past. Instead, You be the only one to ward off his

---

[144] *Bihar al-Anwar*, vol. 74, p. 94.

[145] In the past, deer skin would sometimes be used as paper as it was durable and lasting.

[146] Meaning write your name and your father's name.

[147] Meaning that You help him instead of leaving him at the mercy of the people.

> troubles and fully take care of him. See what is best for him in all of his matters, for if You submit him to Your creation they will not benefit him, and if you give him no option but to resort to his family then they will deny him, and even if they give him, they will give him that which is meager and frustrating, and if they deprive him they will deprive him a lot, and if they be stingy with him, then they are the people of stinginess. O my dear Lord, enrich so and so person son/daughter of so and so person from Your favors, and do not keep him away from Your favors, for he is distressed and has no one other than You, and he is in need of what You have in Your hands, and You do not stand in need of him, and you are aware of him and knowledgeable about him. 'Whoever puts their trust in Allah, He shall suffice him. Surely Allah brings about what He decrees; Allah has set a measure for everything.'[148] 'Indeed with hardship comes ease.'[149] 'Whoever fears Allah, He will find a way out for him, and will provide him with sustenance from where he never even imagines.'[150 and 151]

The first attribute of the believers is to believe in the unseen, and then they are described as establishing the prayer and paying charity.[152]

Allah, the Almighty, is the sole Creator and Sustainer, and He has assigned ways for receiving sustenance and making a living, some of which are material, natural ways and some are spiritual, metaphysical ways. Thus, is there room to find these numerous narrations which mention ways (such as the abovementioned narration) to open the closed doors of sustenance, strange and

---

[148] *Quran*, Surah al-Talaq (65) verse 3.

[149] *Quran*, Surah al-Inshirah (94) verse 6.

[150] *Quran*, Surah al-Talaq (65) verses 2-3.

[151] Source for this narration is *Manhaj al-Da'awat*, p. 126.

[152] This is a reference to Surah al-Baqarah (2), verse 3.

unbelievable?

Abandon Damaging Matters and Impoverishing Habits

Sa'eed ibn Alaqa says that in regards to those thing which bring about poverty:

I heard the Commander of the Faithful Imam Ali (a) say:

1. Leaving spider webs in the house;
2. Urinating in the bath or shower[153];
3. Eating while in the state of ritual impurity (*janabah*)[154];
4. Flossing the teeth with wood;
5. Combing one's hair while standing;
6. Keeping trash inside the house;
7. Making false oaths in God;
8. Adultery;
9. Exhibiting avarice or greed;
10. Sleeping between the sunset (*maghrib*) prayer and the night (*isha*)[155] prayer;
11. Sleeping right before sunrise;
12. Not managing one's expenses;
13. Severing ties with one's kin;
14. Having the habit of lying;
15. Listening to songs/music a lot;

[153] This generally refers to public baths in the past, not toilets.

[154] One becomes in this state after intercourse or ejaculation. One must take a ritual shower to come out of this state.

[155] The time of the sunset (*maghrib*) prayer is shortly after sunset, and the time for the night (*isha'*) prayer is when the sky darkens and the stars become visible, usually 1-2 hours after sunset.

16. Refusing (to help) a male[156] who asks or begs at night (for something).

There are several important points here:

1. Some of these factors which lead to poverty are unseen, metaphysical factors; and others are material, natural factors; while some are a combination of these two.
2. These factors which lead to poverty are conditional, not unrestricted, which means that certain conditions must be met for these factors to have an impact. Furthermore, the "Principle of Conflict"[157] is highly applicable here, and the more important case is given preference. Therefore, it could be the case that one of the factors which brings about poverty is opposed by another factor or other factors which bring about richness, and the latter factor is more powerful or

[156] The Imam (a) mentions a male specifically probably because it was inappropriate for women to beg or ask for money at night, and therefore one was not encouraged to help women at night because usually a woman who would go out in the streets at night during those days was up to no good. One should help them during the day, as it is more appropriate.

[157] In the Science of Jurisprudence (*Usul al-Fiqh*), there is a section dedicated to the issue of "*tazahom*" or "Principle of Conflict." In this section, it is discussed that when there are two conflicting jurisprudential cases, how is the conflict resolved? Further, which of the cases is given preference or priority? For example, assume that a person is drowning. Saving a drowning person is an Islamic obligation. However, to get to the river and save this person, one would have to trespass and walk on private property, and the owner of that property does not grant anyone permission to trespass his property; therefore, it is prohibited to walk there. However, this scenario presents a conflict because on the one hand, one has to save that person, but on the other hand, one is not allowed to trespass. Here the "Principle of Conflict" applies, and scholars of jurisprudence determine that the obligation of saving a drowning person is more important, from a religious perspective, than trespassing. Thus, preference is given to the former, not the latter, and so the Islamic legal verdict is that one must save the drowning person.

important than the former factor. Therefore, the latter factor which brings about richness takes precedence over the factor which brings about poverty, and for this reason the person becomes rich (even though he has committed an act which brings about poverty) and vice-versa. Thus, one should not object how is it that Imam Ali (a) in the abovementioned narrations states that these acts cause poverty when we often see that in reality this is not the case?

This also becomes clear when we examine scientific expressions and common expressions which people use. For example, a doctor says that so and so medicine cures so and so disease, but we observe that many times the patient takes that medicine but is not cured. That is because taking medicine will only provide cure conditionally, as there are many conditions which must be observed, and there are many barriers or conflicts which must be removed for the medicine to provide its effect.

Let us take fire as another example. It is undoubtedly correct to say that fire burns, but this does not mean that certain conditions must be met for the fire to burn, such as contact with the object (for if a fire is far enough, it will not burn). It also does not mean that if there are no barriers or obstacles, and the object is glazed or coated with a chemical substance that prevents the fire from coming into direct contact with the object, then it will not get burned.

Some of these causes of poverty are unlawful and prohibited, such as adultery, severing family ties, engaging with music, lying, and making false oaths, and some of them are un-recommended or undesirable causes, such as the other causes mentioned in the *hadith.*

These unlawful or not recommended causes come in varying degrees, as some of them are more powerful and swift in bringing about poverty, while others are weaker and slower in causing poverty.

Discussing every one of these factors—the economic logic

behind them, their chemical, physical or medical effects on one's mind and nervous system, and also their psychological and economic impact—requires a separate discussion and analysis. May Allah give us the ability to address them in the future.

Perform Beneficial Activities and Comprehensive Acts of Worship

After explaining what causes poverty, Imam Ali (a) said:

> Shall I inform you about what increases sustenance?

They said:

> Yes, O Commander of the Faithful.

The Imam said:

1. Combining the (daily) prayers[158];
2. *Ta'qeeb*[159] after the morning prayer and the afternoon prayer;
3. Keeping ties with one's kin;
4. Cleaning the front yard of your house[160];
5. Being empathetic to one's brother in the way of Allah;
6. Setting out early to work;
7. Seeking Allah's forgiveness;
8. Being trustworthy;
9. Saying the truth;
10. Repeating the *adhaan* when it is called[161];

---

[158] Combining the noon (*zuhr*) and afternoon (*asr*) prayers, and the sunset (*maghrib*) and night (*isha'*) prayers.

[159] *Nawafil* is a set of recommended prayers to be recited after the five daily obligatory prayers.

[160] In old, traditional homes, there used to be an open yard inside the house before entering the rooms. This is called *finaa'* in Arabic.

[161] It is recommended, when hearing the *adhaan* (the call to prayer), to repeat it.

11. Avoiding talking while one is in the bathroom on the toilet;
12. Avoiding greed;
13. Thanking the giver[162];
14. Avoid making false oaths in Allah;
15. Performing ablution (*wudhu'*) before eating;
16. Eating food which falls on the table[163];
17. Whoever glorifies Allah (by saying *Subhanallah*) thirty times a day, Allah will protect him from seventy types of difficulties, the least of them being poverty.[164]

The above factors mentioned fall into four categories[165]:

1. Factors that concern a person's relationship with his Creator, such as combining the prayers, observing the *ta'qeeb* after the prayers and so on. Since Allah is the source of all sustenance, observing these factors will ensure the continuation of Allah's mercy, and will bring about His sustenance to His servants.
2. Factors that concern a person's relationship with the society, such as keeping ties with one's kin, showing empathy, saying the truth and so on.
3. Factors that concern a person's relationship with the environment, such as cleaning one's front yard, not speaking in the toilet, performing ablution before eating and so on.

---

[162] The ultimate giver is Allah, as He bestows everything on us; but it is also recommended to thank anyone who does us a favor.

[163] This means that food should not be wasted, so if a loaf of bread falls off the table, then one should not throw it in the trash. It should be cleaned and consumed.

[164] *Al-Khisaal*, vol. 2, p. 504, hadith no. 2.

[165] These four categories that apply to the factors which increase sustenance also apply to the factors which cause poverty.

4. Factors that directly concern the economy, such as setting out to work early in the morning, being financially trustworthy or being trustworthy in general, and so on.

Section Three

Factors which Cause the Squandering of Wealth and Halting the Causes of Poverty[166]

There are many factors which lead to the destruction of wealth and richness, and they lead to a rise in the rate of poverty either directly or indirectly, such as a hike in prices and the trend or phenomenon of rising costs.[167] The following is a number

---

[166] This chapter will address how to halt the factors which lead to the persistence of poverty. As for halting the factors which lead to the creation of poverty, the first chapter addressed that.

[167] Factors which lead to the destruction of wealth, such as gambling, being wasteful, squandering; and factors which lead to poverty such as the government's ownership and hoarding of public lands and minerals, are among the primary causes of large sections of society becoming poor.

Another factor is the large number of employees, for that transforms thousands, or in some countries millions, of people from being producers to being consumers, and this lowers general production and lays the burden of the employees on the people because their salaries will come from taxes and the like.

Generally speaking, the factors discussed in this chapter fall under these two types (factors which destroy wealth and factors which create poverty).

It is possible to classify these factors in another way: Factors which lead to the destruction of wealth are individual factors; and factors which lead to poverty are general factors that are influenced by governments, and the fifteen factors which will be discussed. Companies and small institutions fall under the category of individual factors; and multinational companies fall under the category of governments due to the sheer size of their impact.

of significant direct and indirect factors which lead to the destruction of wealth and richness:

State Ownership

State ownership of natural resources such as land, minerals, forests, and oceans and their resources clearly cause poverty and deprivation. It also causes a rise in prices because if land and other resources were freely available for all people, then a great financial burden would be lifted from the poor, and the rates of poverty would automatically drop. Furthermore, the poor would have greater opportunities and easier access to becoming wealthy in a legitimate way.

Islam emphasizes that the sources of wealth all belong to Allah, and then they are for the people. A state has no right to deny anyone from owning some of those sources.

Allah mentions in the Quran:

> It is He Who created for you all that is in the earth.[168]

Prophet Muhammad (s) said:

> Whoever is first to own something not owned by another Muslim, is entitled to it.[169]

Imam Ali (a) granted people the freedom and the full right to farm and develop any land they desired, to construct what they desired, to pasture what they desired, to invest in, and possess any part of the forest or minerals that they desired.[170]

Having too many Employees

Islam views having too many employees in government offices and institutions a burden on the poor, as these employees live and

---

[168] *Quran*, Surah al-Baqarah (2) verse 29.

[169] *Mustadrak al-Wasa'il*, vol. 17, p. 111.

[170] Refer to the book, *al-Siyasah min Waqe' al-Islam* and the book, *The Government of Prophet Muhammad (s) and the Commander of the Faithful Imam Ali (a)*.

consume without any production. The poor on the other hand, have to strive very hard to produce, but they barely are able to consume and have what they want. This is a widespread and common problem in countries governed by the closed economy of the state. Here are some examples:

1. Thousands of employees and workers in the military, police and intelligence bureaus.
2. Thousands of employees and workers in immigration, citizenship, and passport offices, in addition to border posts.
3. Thousands of employees in offices and institutions run by government ministries.

Imam Ali (a) undertook an astonishing task in reducing the number of government employees. With strategic planning that was politically, economically, and administratively comprehensive and complete, he managed to establish justice in Kufa—a city of four million residents—with only one judge!

Similarly, after the Conquest of Mecca,[171] Prophet Muhammad (s) appointed a single person, named Otab, to govern Mecca, even though Mecca was the center of opposition against the Prophet (s) for decades, and it was filled with armed resistance.[172]

Arms Race

The arms races annually exhausts billions of dollars which are not really necessary for the security and defense of nations. According to a report prepared by the Peace Research Institute, military expenses for the year 2004 exceeded one trillion dollars!

---

[171] It was a peaceful conquest in AD 630. The Prophet (s) issued general amnesty to all Meccans and not a single drop of blood was spilled.

[172] For further insight on the drawbacks of having too many government employees, refer to the following books: *al-Siyaghah al-Jadidah*, *The Jurisprudence of the Islamic Government*, and the book, *The Jurisprudence of the Judiciary*, all authored by the late Imam al-Shirazi. Also refer to the book, *The Government of the Messenger (s)* by Dr. Mohsen al-Musawi.

In 2006, military spending reached 2.8 trillion dollars!

It is quite evident that instead of spending these very large figures on providing basic needs for people, they were spent on devices and tools that cause death and on weapons of mass destruction. Furthermore, weapons have negative consequences, such as the following:

1. Weapons represent a big burden on people as the government uses tax money to produce and buy them. This creates an additional burden on the poor. Sometimes the government uses money that the state makes or money generated from natural resources such as oil to fund its weapons program. This means that the state is stealing the wealth of the people in the name of defense and national security, and in the name of ensuring the survival of the ruling dictatorial regime or even the dictatorial regime guised in democracy.

2. These weapons easily find their way to domestic conflicts and wars. Sometimes even arms dealers and weapons companies from around the globe, in addition to countries that manufacture weapons, plan to instigate wars either directly or through proxies in order to market their weapons. They also make an effort to continue and drag these wars on for years and years. Wars, in reality, cause the mass destruction of cities and territories, and they represent one of the leading causes of poverty. The late Imam al-Shirazi (may Allah have mercy on him) explains that the awaited savior Imam al-Mahdi (a) might replace modern weapons and military techniques with ancient weapons and military techniques, such as the sword and the spear as an example. This means that first, all of the money spent on modern weapons will be saved and allocated to the people and the poor. Second, the danger and destruction of wars caused by political, social or economic motives will significantly decrease to less than one

in a hundred thousand![173]

Government Theft

Theft can be masked[174] or unmasked. This is a long discussion which we defer to another occasion, but here it suffices us to give the following example.

A student of Imam Ali (a), Abu Dharr al-Ghifari objected to Mu'awiya when he had a palace which cost four million golden *dinars* built for him! Abu Dharr told him:

> If you built this palace of yours with Allah's money, then you have committed a sin and a prohibited act; and if you have built it with your own money, then you have wasted your money and become extravagant!

Lack of Proper Distribution (or Mismanagement)

Allah the Almighty is the Creator of the entire earth, and He created all of humanity. He has assigned the earth and all of its resources for all people, as He explicitly says in the Quran:

> It is He Who created for you all that is in the earth."[175]

This means that everything on the earth is for everyone. People however, due to their ignorance, divided the world and imposed geographic borders, resulting in some nations being rich with resources, while other nations suffer from lack of adequate resources.[176]

---

[173] Refer to the book *Imam al-Mahdi*, may Allah hasten his reappearance, by Imam al-Shirazi.

[174] Examples of masked theft is (unjust) taxes and selling what is owned by the people, such as the sale of oil and natural gas by oil countries to the people, even though these resources belong to the people.

[175] *Quran*, Surah al-Baqarah (2) verse 29.

[176] The Global Risk Report in 2012, published by the World Economic Forum that was conducted in Davos-Klosters, Switzerland, revealed that the greatest economic threats facing the world are: major income inequality and the unstable financial state of governments.

Geographic borders present double harm. On the one hand, they deprive poor territories or countries from resources to which they were entitled according to the law of God. On the other hand, they prevent free economic activity and trade between countries. Instead, these borders result in customs or tariffs that harm the poor in both countries.

Thus, we see that Prophet Muhammad (s) eliminated geographic borders between the nine countries which were ruled by his government.

Imam Ali (a) also eliminated geographic borders between the fifty countries which were ruled by his government. Similarly, Imam al-Mahdi (a) will eliminate all of the geographic borders of the world when he reappears at the end of time, thereby "filling the earth with justice and equity just as it had been filled with oppression and injustice."[177]

---

[177] The late Grand Ayatollah Imam Sayed Mohammad al-Shirazi states in his book *The 21st Century and the Revival of Life:* "Currently, geographic borders must be lifted from all countries, not only from the Muslim countries. That is because geographic borders make humans less worthy than cockroaches, rats, birds and animals, for are there borders barring these creatures? Do they not walk and fly as they wish, and do the fish not swim wherever they want? But the West, however, has limited the human being and imposed shackles upon him with citizenship and residency requirements, thereby constricting his movements and activities and preventing him from realizing his goals. We see that every country has borders, and one is not permitted to cross those borders except with a passport or an entry permit. To the contrary, we see that the great Messenger, Prophet Muhammad (s), abolished all of the borders between Muslim countries. Therefore, wherever a Muslim resided at that time, he would be in his country and in his homeland. Some might wrongly assume that the lifting of borders will lead to crime and chaos, but that is not the case (as history reveals that chaos and crime did not ensue when the borders were properly lifted in many parts of the world. The European Union is a recent example. Was there chaos when borders were practically removed between the member states?) Imposing borders violates humanity, violates rationality, and violates human dignity. Borders

Gambling

Almighty Allah states:

> They ask you about wine and games of chance (gambling). Say: In both of these there is great evil, even though there is some benefit for people, but their evil is greater than their benefit.[178]

Gambling is one of the primary factors that destroy the social foundation of the poor and family life. This in turn, reflects negatively on production because gambling represents absolute consumption. The gambler does not produce anything, as he simply lives on the pockets of others! There are details about this issue which are found in specialized books.[179]

Financial Corruption

Imam Ali (a) states:

> Those who perished before you perished because they denied people their rights so they had to buy them, and they took people by falsehood and they followed them.[180]

---

were imposed due to the ignorance of the rulers who intended to limit the human being. Now that the horizons of knowledge have broadened, there is a greater awareness, and most dictatorial regimes have faded, it is necessary for those borders to fade as well. Borders were imposed during the harshest times of the colonial rule, and now that colonial rule has ended, those borders must end too."

[178] *Quran*, Surah al-Baqarah (2) verse 219.

[179] A report released by Annabaa Information Network, entitled "Gambling: The Progressing Cancer of Western Civilization," said that the West is filled with official places for corruption, immorality, prostitution, and money laundering in indirect ways. With advanced technology, those who visit or market such places now have huge capabilities to attract clients, visitors and investors from all over the world, whether through normal channels, through the internet, or through special companies.

[180] *Nahj al-Balagha*, p. 366, letter 79.

In another narration he says:

> It is not acceptable for a governor who takes bribes to be in power, for he will take away the rights (of the people) and fall short of observing their due rights.[181]

Bribery makes the poor poorer. It is a form of exploitation, corruption, cheating and depravity. One who takes bribes exploits the needs of his subjects, whether they are poor or rich, thereby increasing the rate and degree of poverty in both instances. As for the rich, they will compensate for their losses incurred by bribes by increasing the price of their products and merchandise.[182]

Monopolization[183]

Prophet Muhammad (s) said:

> A person who releases his products for sale will be given sustenance, and the one who hoards them will be cursed.[184]

Imam Ali (a) says in his letter to Malik al-Ashtar:

> Ban monopolization (or hoarding), for the Messenger of Allah (s) banned it. Let the sales be generous or flexible, based on the standards of justice. Prices should not be unjust to either of the parties, the seller and the buyer.[185]

In numerous narrations, Imam Ali (a) directs us to the essence

---

[181] *Nahj al-Balagha*, sermon 131.

[182] The Global Corruption Report of 2009, prepared by Transparency International, revealed that the world annually spends between 20 to 40 billion dollars on bribes. This amount is equivalent to about 20-40% of official development benefits or donations. This inflicts harm on commerce, business, development and consumers.

[183] Monopolization is to hoard food or whatever people require in times of need, or whatever is scarce so that the prices rise and then one offers his goods for sale.

[184] *Al-Kafi*, by al-Kulayni, vol. 5, p. 165.

[185] *Nahj al-Balagha*, vol. 3, letter 53.

of monopolization and its limits. He points out the reality of the hoarder and his psychological makeup. Very briefly, we shall mention a few of his words in this regard.

In one narration, Imam Ali (a) says:

> In good economic conditions, the limit for hoarding is forty days, and in times of economic hardship, the limit is three days. Whoever exceeds these limits is cursed.[186]

Monopolization or hoarding is an omen on any society and on the one who practices it as well. Therefore, the one who practices it is cursed, meaning that he is expelled from Allah's mercy and away from goodness and blessings.

As for the Imam stating forty days as a limit during good economic times and three days as a limit in times of economic hardship, it could be due to external factors during that time and not a set or fixed law to be applied everywhere and in all eras. This matter depends on the circumstances of a given time, and so the limit can either decrease or increase. The task of determining it will rest on the ruler who fulfills the conditions of satisfying Allah and also satisfying the people based on the criteria that my late father has laid out in his book *al-Shura fi al-Islam* (Consultation in Islam) and *Al-Fiqh: al-Dawla al-Islamiyya* (The Law of the Islamic Government), in addition to other books.

In another hadith, Imam Ali (a) states:

> Hoarding is the habit or nature (*sheema* in Arabic) of the immoral ones.[187]

A society is comprised of groups, and each group has psychological characteristics or certain habits. The word "*sheema*" in Arabic (which Imam Ali (a) uses) means one's nature or disposition. The immoral ones (*fujjar* in Arabic, which Imam Ali used in this tradition) have a particular psychological makeup, a particular ideological structure, and a particular narrow-mindedness.

---

[186] *Da'aim al-Islam*, vol. 2, p. 36. Also refer to *al-Kafi*, vol. 5, p. 165.

[187] *Ghurar al-Hikam*, vol. 1, p. 33. *Mustadrak al-Wasa'il*, vol. 13, p. 276.

Hoarding is considered to be one of the manifestations of the psychological makeup of the immoral ones. Therefore, it is possible to know the personality and psychological makeup of a person who hoards from one's act of hoarding!

Imam Ali (a) also says:

> The one who hoards is deprived of one's blessings.[188]

The one who hoards is deprived of blessings even if one makes profit and one's stocks pile up because he loses his dignity and the purity of his conscience. He also loses his reputation among the people and position in society. Thus, one loses the "blessing" itself because it transforms into a curse as a result of one's hoarding. To further elaborate:

1. Instead of benefitting from one's blessings (i.e. his goods or merchandise) for his worldly life by increasing the flow and circulation of his capital and goods, which serves to stimulate the economy and earn one profits, you find him hoarding and amassing his goods. Consequently, his goods become frozen and stagnant, and in turn, he also freezes and stagnates. He and his goods will become like standing water, the more it stays still, the moldier it will become.
2. Instead of benefitting from one's blessings for the hereafter by spending one's money for charitable causes, helping others, establishing institutions and other righteous projects, you find him hoarding his wealth and the blessings that God endowed him with. Thus, one is truly deprived from one's blessings.

Imam Ali (a) also says:

> A stingy hoarder amasses for one who will not be grateful to him (such as his inheritors), and one will be on the way

[188] *Ghurar al-Hikam*, vol. 1, p. 33. Also see *Mustadrak al-Wasa'il*, vol. 13, p. 276.

> to meet the One (God) who will not excuse him.[189]

The "futuristic outlook" condemns the stingy hoarder because he bequeaths his wealth to his children and other inheritors. His inheritors quickly forget him and become consumed with using and squandering his wealth to fulfill their desires. It is quite rare to find them adhering to the straight path, and even if they do, they will not praise their father who used to hoard his wealth.

Instead, they will be disgraced by such a father or even embarrassed by him, surely how could they be grateful to him? In addition to all of that, this stingy hoarder will meet his destiny in the hereafter by having to answer to the One who will not excuse him either - so is there a loser more at loss than this person?

Interest (Usury)

Almighty Allah states in the Holy Quran:

> Allah deprives interest (usury) of all blessings, whereas He blesses charity with growth.[190]

Imam Ali (a) says:

> O businessmen! Learn your religion and then do business. Learn your religion and then do business, for I swear by Allah that interest (usury) in this nation is more discreet than the walking of an ant on a rock.[191]

This is a reference to discreet forms of interest or taking interest with deception.

So how does interest spread the disease of poverty in the body of a nation? We will point out two ways out of the many, in which getting a loan leads to creating poverty:

1. The person who seeks a loan is in desperate need of money,

[189] *Ghurar al-Hikam*, vol. 1, p. 93, ch. 1, trad. 1865.

[190] *Quran*, Surah al-Baqarah (2) verse 276.

[191] *Tahdhib al-Ahkam*, vol. 7, p. 6, ch. 1, trad. 16.

such as needing it to undergo a surgery or seeking immediate medical treatment. Other examples are needing money to pay for the cost of one's son's wedding, repaying a debt, paying taxes or a fine, and so on. It is obvious that such a person has limited income, otherwise one would not be desperate to seek a loan. Therefore, taking interest from them, even if the interest is low, serves to add more pressure upon them and increase their state of poverty; or it serves to downgrade them from the middle class to a lower class.

2. A person may seek a loan to start a business or expand one's business. It is obvious that taking interest from this investor in the end generates pressure on the poor as well because the investor will reduce the wages of his employees, who usually have a limited income, to compensate for the interest imposed upon him. Or the investor might increase the price of his products, all of which will reflect negatively on the poor. Furthermore, interest creates an unproductive group in society because this easy way of making money will drive many people to deal with interest. This phenomenon will start from a small village and spread to global levels.

   Therefore, a group of unproductive people will be created because this group will make money by sucking the blood of others, thereby increasing the gap between the rich and the poor. The rich will become richer, and the poor will become poorer. Consequently, a number of social problems will also be created in the short term and in the long term. In the short gterm, the economic pressure incurred by interest will destroy the family and create psychological illnesses such as depression and stress, in addition to causing a range of other health issues. All of this will directly and negatively impact production, and the poor will become poorer from several aspects.

   Recently, Japan came to realize the great harms of interest, so it decreased the rate of interest all the way down close to zero, and then it ultimately reduced it down to zero. To the contrary, banning interest will push for real and fruitful production, such as agriculture, development and construction. In other words, interest transforms money from a healthy means of exchanging goods to a "fake product."[192]

When Hisham ibn al-Hakam asked Imam al-Sadiq (a) about the reason why Islam outlaws interest, Imam al-Sadiq (a) referred to some of the points that we have mentioned here. The Imam said to him:

> If usury was allowed (Islamically legal), then people (meaning most people) would have abandoned trading and doing business. Hence, Allah outlawed usury so

---

[192] The late Grand Ayatollah Imam Sayed Mohammad al-Shirazi states in his book *Fiqh al-Awlama* (The Jurisprudence of Globalization): "What distinguishes Islamic globalization materialistically and financially is the lack of interest (usury), for it is the distinguishing feature of an Islamic economy, such that the owner of capital does not oppress and is not oppressed (as Allah states in the Quran). This non-interest feature is among the sources of pride and unique properties of this divine and sound economy, and this is how it is distinguished from the capitalist economy and the short-lived communist and socialist economy. Many banks around the world have adopted the theory of the non-interest bank in Islam, which is essentially a contributory bank that does not oppress its clients or customers. Instead, both of them share profits or share losses, depending on market fluctuations."

The late Imam al-Shirazi also added: "Interest and interest based transactions are prohibited. Imam Ali Ibn Musa al-Ridha (a) wrote to Muhammad ibn Sinaan: 'The reason why Allah prohibited interest is because of the financial corruption that it causes. If a person buys one dirham for two *dirhams*, the price of a *dirham* is a *dirham*, and so the price of the other *dirham* is false. Therefore, dealing in interest is a loss for the buyer and the seller. That is why Allah outlawed interest due to the financial corruption that it involves. Just like Allah has banned the foolish ones from managing his finances because of the concern that he might waste his money, until he matures; for this reason Allah has prohibited interest, and selling interest is selling a *dirham* for two dirhams...'"

> people would keep away from usury and instead resort to trading, buying and selling. Then they would (help each other) by giving loans.[193]

Polluting the Environment

One of the leading causes of poverty is harming the environment, and Allah has warned about that by saying:

> And when he attains authority, he goes about the earth spreading mischief and destroying crops and human life, and Allah does not love mischief.[194]

Both governments and people collaborate in polluting or destroying the environment. As for governments, they are the primary cause of destroying the environment, and here are a couple of examples for that:

1. The refusal of the United States to ratify the Kyoto Protocol which commits states to reduce greenhouse emissions that cause great harm to the layer of ozone.
2. The nuclear reactor in the former Soviet Union, known as the Chernobyl disaster (it was a nuclear meltdown in 1986 which severely affected the environment until this day).[195]

---

[193] *Man La Yahdhurah al-Faqih*, vol. 3, p. 567. In a report published by Annabaa Information Network, it seems that many economists, after the global financial crisis, have considered the Islamic financial system to be the only system possible that prevents such a recurring crisis. Western governments essentially nationalizing (or bailing out) failing corporations represent a fall back on the principles and foundations of capitalist economy, demonstrating the end of that era.

[194] *Quran*, Surah al-Baqarah (2) verse 205.

[195] A study said that the deterioration of the environment can push nearly 50 million people to be displaced from their hometowns by 2010. The world needs to define a new type of asylum called the "environmental refugee." This study, prepared by the Institute of Environment and Human Security at the United Nations University, revealed that desertification, rising seawater, floods, and storms induced by climate

The people are also responsible for damaging the environment. It is obvious that damaging the environment makes the poor poorer and downgrades the middle class groups to the lower class. This is because damaging the environment is among the leading causes of disease, and disease is among the leading causes of poverty for the following reasons:

1. Disease prevents a worker or employee from being productive, and so the family is deprived from the earnings of its breadwinner.
2. Disease imposes huge financial burdens on a family, and often times even middle class families are incapable of bearing such a responsibilities.

Damaging the environment also harms agriculture, which in turn negatively reflects on the poor. For further details, refer to the book *al-Fiqh al-Bee'ah* (*The Law of the Environment*) by the late Imam al-Shirazi.

Wasting and Squandering

Almighty Allah states in the Quran:

> Verily, those who squander wastefully are the brothers of Satan.[196]

Imam Ali (a) says:

> Squandering is the path to becoming needy.[197]

If you want to become in need of others, stretching your hands to them and begging them to give you from the leftover of their tables, then all you need to do is squander your wealth and spend

---

change may lead to the displacement of hundreds of millions of people. It estimated that some 20 million were indeed forced to migrate due to problems caused by the destruction of the environment, such as the erosion of agricultural lands and contamination of water.

[196] *Quran*, Surah al-Isra' (17) verse 27.

[197] *Ghurar al-Hikam*, hadith no. 8,135.

it on parties, unnecessary food, unnecessary travels and other luxuries.

Imam Ali (a) says:

> The person who boasts by squandering wastefully will become humiliated by bankruptcy.[198]

The Imam (a) says in another *hadith*:

> Be generous, but do not squander; and be economic, but do not be stingy.[199]

Without a doubt, so many resources are being wasted in the world today and when we refer to the sayings in Islam, we see that Imam Ali (a) says:

> Do not waste, for people (and Allah) will not appreciate or praise the generosity of the one who wastes, nor will they have mercy on his poverty."

This amazing narration not only discourages one from wasting, but it also explains the reason why one should not be wasteful. The reason is that a wasteful person who aimlessly spends will not be praised or commended for being generous. At the same time, when he becomes poor because of his wasteful spending, Allah will not have mercy on him, and the people will also not have mercy on him because they will blame him for his poverty due to his wasteful behavior.

In another narration, Imam Ali (a) says:

> The cause of poverty is squandering.[200]

This *hadith* is quite clear that being wasteful is a cause of poverty, and the generality of this *hadith* means that this applies to individuals, groups and governments. Just see how much the governments waste!

---

[198] Ibid., hadith no. 8,141.

[199] *Nahj al-Balagha*, maxim 33.

[200] *Ghurar al-Hikam*, vol. 1, p. 390, ch. 38, trad. 20.

Imam Ali (a) says in yet another *hadith*:

> The highest honor is to abstain from squandering and wasting.[201]

Therefore, a person who does not even discard the seed of a fruit if there is still some fruit left on it to eat is indeed an honorable person; the one who shuts off the water while performing the various actions of the ablution is an honorable person; the one who turns off the lights when they are not needed is an honorable person; the one who does not discard used appliances, clothes and furniture in the garbage is an honorable person - even debris or rubble is not to be wasted if one can find a use for it or sell it! All of these are considered to be the highest honor.

In another *hadith*, Imam Ali (a) states:

> Woe upon the extravagant or wasteful person! How far is he from being upright and soundly managing his affairs![202]

This means that squandering and uprightness are completely the opposite of each other (meaning that in no case is squandering a good thing). It also means that a person who is wasteful is shortsighted and careless about the consequences of his actions.

The Exception of Excessive Spending on Charitable Causes

Imam Ali (a) says:

> Excessive spending is objectionable in everything except in acts of goodness.[203]

The philosophy behind this exception is that "acts of goodness" generate economic, social and psychological benefits—in addition to the benefits in the hereafter—for a person who gives.

The one who generously gives for charitable causes such

[201] Ibid., vol. 2, p. 256, ch. 78, trad. 138.

[202] Ibid., vol. 2, p. 303, ch. 83, trad. 31.

[203] Ibid., vol. 1, p. 101, ch. 1, trad. 1960.

as giving to the poor, orphans, establishing mosques, schools, libraries, Husayniyyas, academies, research institutions, universities and seminaries - gains the trust of people and their admiration. Therefore, all people extend to him their hand of support, and they would not allow his businesses to collapse and fail. Even if his businesses fail, everyone will try to lift him and support him in any way or method, thereby making him stronger than he was before.

Therefore, Imam Ali (a) also said:

> Excessive spending is objectionable in everything except in acts of goodness and in exerting a great effort in the obedience (of God).[204]

It is possible to say that the Imam did not really make an exception in the abovementioned *hadith*. The tradition says "excessive spending" (*israaf* in Arabic), but in reality when one uses the money of God to spend it in God's way and obedience, then this is not considered "excessive spending" or squandering. In other words, there is no such thing as "excessive spending" or "squandering" when it comes to acts of goodness and charitable causes.

Therefore, the exception that Imam Ali (a) makes (by saying excessive spending is objectionable except in acts of goodness) is not really an exception (but it is simply a literary tool that he employs to convey the importance of giving to charitable causes).

In any case, there is nothing strange about the two abovementioned *ahadith* (which encourage excessive spending for charitable causes) because they are in sync with the Holy Quran which states:

> They even prefer them (meaning others) above themselves though poverty be their own lot.[205]

It is also possible that the Imam (a) made the exception in order

[204] Ibid., vol. 2, p. 56, ch. 58, trad. 85.

[205] *Quran*, Surah al-Hashr (59) verse 9.

to create a balance (as people usually do not give much for charitable causes, so they are encouraged to give "excessively" so that they at least give moderately, but if they are instructed to give moderately, then they will give only meagerly).

Cheating and Defrauding

Almighty Allah states in the Holy Quran:

> Woe to the defrauders. Those who when they take the measure from people demand it full. But when they measure out to others or weight out for them, they give them less than due.[206]

One narration says:

> Whenever the goods of others are diminished when taking measure, then poverty and loss will emerge.[207]

In another verse of the Quran, the Almighty Allah states:

> Therefore, give full measure and weight and do not diminish to people their things, and do not make mischief in the land after it has been set in order.[208]

This (defrauding) is what governments and many businessmen do these days, and it is one of the causes of poverty because defrauding people reflects negatively especially on those who have limited income. In addition, cheating and defrauding apply direct pressure on the poor.

Hence, we see that Imam al-Baqir (a) prohibited Hisham from selling the "*sabiri*," which is an expensive type of cloth, in the shade (because it is dark and cannot be seen well). The Imam (a) said to him:

> O Hisham, selling it in the shade is cheating, and cheating

[206] *Quran*, Surah al-Mutaffifeen (83) verses 1-3.

[207] *Mustadrak al-Wasa'il*, vol. 13, p. 234. Also refer to *Jame' Ahadith al-Shia*, vol. 13, p. 410.

[208] *Quran*, Surah al-A'raaf (7) verse 85.

> is not permissible.[209]

Among the recommendations of Imam al-Sadiq (a), he said:

> Do not conceal the defects (of your products) in your transactions. Do not cheat the one who is unaware (does not have an idea of prices), for cheating a person is unlawful. Do not accept for people except what you accept for yourself. Give people their rights and take your rights, but do not betray and have no fear.[210]

It is obvious that not concealing the defects of products and not cheating those who are naïve has a direct impact on easing the pressure on the poor. It also has an indirect impact by spreading trust among the people, which reflects positively on social relations and eases social unrest and agitation, all of which serve to provide a foundation for a solid and thriving economy. Furthermore, it drives people to perfect their products instead of cheating and playing with the measures.

Perfecting products improves their quality and increases their longevity, thereby easing the pressure on others since they will not have to rebuy the same product after a short period of time due to the product becoming defective or faulty.

Counterfeiting Currency

One of the causes of poverty and rising prices is counterfeiting currency because printing more more than what the currency is backed by leads to inflation.

We see that once, when Imam al-Kadhim (a) looked at a *dinar* (golden coin) and realized that it was not pure (as it was mixed with other metals), he took it in his hands and cut it in half. Then he said:

> Throw it down the drain so that nothing fake or counterfeit is sold.

---

[209] *Tahdhib al-Ahkam*, vol. 7, p. 13.

[210] *Wasa'il al-Shia*, vol. 17, p. 385.

This act sent an important message to all of those who counterfeit money.

Imam Ali (a), when talking about immoral scholars also similarly said:

> They cast nets for people made from the ropes of deception and words of falsehood.

In another *hadith*, Imam Ali (a) also said:

> The money of Muslims cannot sustain any harm or damage.[211]

Imposing Taxes on Consumption

Imposing taxes on consumption is a grave mistake that the present day governments are making. Islam on the other hand, places taxes on unused profits. Imposing taxes on consumption applies severe pressure on the poor and adds to their poverty.

We find that in the Western countries, there are taxes on every product, such that everything one buys from the supermarket or mall comes with a tax, thereby creating a greater burden on the poor.[212]

In Islam however, taxes such as *zakat* and *khums* are levied only if one ends up with wealth that exceeds one's needs (such as food, clothing, transportation, housing, marriage costs, and recreation that is appropriate to one's status). In this case, after the passage of an entire year on making a profit,[213] and after excluding all of the expenses and needs, one is to pay 20% of this unused profit.

---

[211] *Al-Khisaal*, p. 310. Also refer to *Wasa'il al-Shia*, vol. 17, p. 404.

[212] A tax on added value is a combined tax imposed on the difference between the cost and the price of the product. This emerged for the first time in France in 1954.

[213] Some scholars state that this tax becomes mandatory after the passage of one year from the beginning of the investment or doing business (not from the beginning of making a profit).

Imam Ali (a) says to Malik al-Ashtar in his letter to him:

> You should keep an eye on the cultivation or development of the land more than on the collection of revenue because revenue cannot be attained without cultivation, and whoever asks for revenue without cultivation ruins the area and brings death to the people. His rule will last for only a moment. If they complain of the heaviness (of the revenue) or of diseases, or dearth of water, or excess of water, or of a change in the condition of the land either due to flood or to drought, then you should remit the revenue to the extent that you hope will improve their position. The remission granted by you for the removal of distress from them should not be grudged by you, because it is an investment which they will return to you in the shape of the prosperity of your country and the progress of your domain, in addition to earning their praise and happiness for meeting out justice to them. You can depend upon their strength because of the investment made by you in them through catering to their convenience, and you can have confidence in them because of the justice extended to them by being kind to them. After that, circumstances may turn such that you have to ask for their assistance, when they will bear it happily, for prosperity is capable of hearing whatever you load on it. The ruin of the land is caused by the poverty of the cultivators, and the cultivators will become poor when the officers concentrate on the collection (of money), having little hope for continuance (in their posts) and deriving no benefit from objects of warning.

Glutting the Market or "Dumping"

Glutting the market or dumping is prohibited in Islam because it poses economic damage on a nation and is considered as unfair competition. It also leads to the closure of factories and the layoffs of workers, it creates social and political unrest, and it also leads to a fall in the gross national product.

Prophet Muhammad (s) said:

> There should be neither harm nor malice.

Imam Ali (a) also said in deterring people from inflicting harm on the general population:

> There is among them—the traders and skilled workers—many who are narrow-minded, awfully avaricious, hoarders of goods for profiteering...and this is a source of harm to the people."

For this reason, the late Imam al-Shirazi (may Allah have mercy on his soul) issued a verdict in his book *al-Fiqh al-Moroor*[214] (*The Law of Traffic*) prohibiting it due to the "Law of No Harm." Dumping or glutting the market is among the most important tools used by colonial powers to destroy developing countries, and it is also among the most important harms to globalization.

[214] Refer to pages 176-177 of the book.

Chapter Two

The Poor: Educating Them, Their Obligations, Responsibilities, and Their Paths to Richness

Prelude

The discussions in this chapter revolve around the following three points:

The first point: A general outlook on the poor will be presented. The education and culture which the poor must enrich themselves with will also be discussed based on what we learn from the teachings of Imam Ali (a).

The second point: Some of the most important obligations of the poor will be discussed here, and by extension, some of the most important responsibilities that the poor have will also be discussed.

The third point: This point will revolve around the ways, methods, tools, and natural means[215] that the poor can and must employ or observe to lift themselves out of poverty.

[215] The natural means are those necessary, natural steps that one must take in order to achieve a particular objective. Once these means are pursued and all necessary conditions are met, then the desired effect or result will be achieved.

It is quite evident that many of these ways and tools, in addition to those obligations and responsibilities, are not confined to the poor, rather they are general and include even the middle class and also the rich.[216] We mention the poor in particular due to their excessive needs.

It is also necessary to note that whatever will be discussed in the point about obligations (of the poor) is also suitable to be discussed in the point about the ways and methods (to be lifted from poverty), and vice-versa, even though some modifications must be made to those points (for them to be suitable to fall under each point). This is because both points contain the aspect of obligations (of the poor) and ways or methods (for the poor to lift themselves up from poverty).

We did not take it upon ourselves to collect all of the teachings of Imam Ali (a) about these three points as that would require authoring a large volume or even more. We simply limited the discussion to very brief pearls and pieces from the Imam's teachings. Furthermore, we based our selection of Imam Ali's (a) words from the book *al-Maal: Akhdhan wa Ata'an wa Sarfan* (Wealth: Taking it, Giving it, and Spending it). This book is part of the *al-Fiqh* (Islamic Law) encyclopedia by my late father. We took some of the narrations that he presented in that book, and we added some commentaries and elaborations to them.

The First Point

The General Outlook on the Poor and the Education and Culture of the Poor

Making a Lawful Living is Worship

In a long hadith by Imam Ali (a), he says that Prophet Muhammad

---

[216] The rich are at risk of becoming poor if they disregard the methods to preserve and protect their wealth. Furthermore, if they do not observe their obligations and fulfill their responsibilities, then their wealth will lead them to misery instead of happiness.

(s) asked his Lord on the Night of Ascension:

> My Lord, which deeds are the most beloved to you? Allah replied to him: O Ahmad, worship has ten parts, and nine of those parts are in earning a lawful living. Therefore, if your food and drink come from a pure, lawful source, then you will be in My protection and side.[217]

There are two questions here:

The first question: How is making a lawful living a form of worship?

Answer: Worship is whatever brings a person closer to the Almighty Allah, and God is the One who instructs us how to worship Him. Just as a servant of God becomes closer to Him through prayer because God loves prayer, in the same way a servant of God becomes closer to Him through making a lawful living because God loves it. Just as a servant of God pursues His satisfaction by praying or going to *hajj* (pilgrimage), he also pursues His satisfaction by following the system, laws and rulings that God Has fixed when it comes to making a living from lawful money, not unlawful money. Just as a servant of God shines with spiritual ascension and becomes closer to Allah by that, he can also shine with financial honesty and purity and become closer to Allah.

The second question: Why is it that worship is ten parts and making a lawful living comprises nine parts of it?

Answer: One of the reasons could be that making an unlawful living is the primary cause of ruining one's Hereafter and also this life. Making an unlawful living could include other vices such as theft in all its forms, deception, cheating, bribery, hoarding, usury, embezzlement and gambling? These vices, among others, destroy the foundations of a society and nation, and they demolish the pillars of civilization. They also put an end to values and moral standards and rob people of their economic

---

217 *Jame' Ahadith al-Shia*, vol. 17, p. 86; *Irshaad al-Qulub*, vol. 1, p. 203.

and social security. Furthermore, the one who makes a lawful living will be able to worship properly. To the contrary, one who makes an unlawful living and buys a house or clothes with unlawful money will not be able to worship correctly because his prayer—which is the pillar of faith—will not even be accepted!

Making a Living is an Obligation

It has been reported that Imam al-Sadiq (a) narrated from his father, from his grandfathers, from Prophet Muhammad (s) saying:

> Making a living is an obligation that comes after the obligation (of prayer).[218]

The most popular or well-known "obligation" is prayer, which is considered to be the pillar of faith and the ascension of a believer. There is also another "obligation" which this *hadith* mentions, and that is the obligation of making a living.

Spending on oneself, their spouse, children, parents and grandfathers—and even grandmothers, as some scholars issue a verdict mandating it (if they are needy), while others consider it an obligatory precaution—is mandatory. In addition, spending on what one owns of animals, whether it is birds, cattle, or other domestic animals, is also mandatory.

One of the Types of Jihad (Struggle) is Economic Struggle

It has been narrated from Musa son of Bakr that he said Abu al-Hasan (a)[219] told me:

> A person who seeks a lawful living to spend it on himself and his family is like the one who fights in the way of Allah, the Almighty. If he is not able to meet his needs, then let him take a loan for the sake of Allah and His

[218] *Bihar al-Anwar*, vol. 100, p. 17, ch. 1, hadith no. 79.

[219] Abu al-Hasan is one of the titles of Imam al-Kadhim (a).

> Messenger to bring food for his family. If he dies before paying his debt, then it is upon the Imam to pay his debt, and if the Imam does not pay it, then he will bear its sin.
>
> The Almighty Allah states in the Quran: The alms are meant only for the poor, the needy, those who are in charge thereof, those whose hearts are to be reconciled, to free those in bondage, and to help those burdened with debt...[220]
>
> Therefore, this person is poor, is needy and is burdened with debt.[221]

What we can take away from this and other *ahadith* is that there is a type of important *jihad* or struggle called "economic struggle."

This type of struggle might not be any less important than a military *jihad* or struggle, meaning to fight the oppressors and transgressors. The reason is that economic struggle ensures the continuation of what is achieved by military struggle, and so it serves to guarantee the continuation of life in a healthy way.

There are two pillars to this struggle:

1. To make a living from legitimate sources;
2. To spend it on establishing a healthy family and managing its affairs, for the family is the primary building block of a society. If the institution of family is healthy, then society will be healthy; but if the family is not healthy or is corrupt, then society will also be corrupt.

Now if someone faces closed doors and cannot meet one's financial obligations, then that person should seek a loan, for seeking a loan is one of the doors of life. After that, one should fulfill his debt, and if he is unable to, then the Muslim Treasury (public funds) should pay it for him. If the Muslim Treasury—which is controlled by governments in our world today—does

[220] *Quran*, Surah al-Tawbah (9) verse 60.

[221] *Al-Kafi*, vol. 5, p. 93, trad. 3.

not pay his debt, then the sin, felony and (Divine) punishment of not paying the debt will rest with those who are in charge of the Muslim Treasury. Everyone who is somehow connected to the Muslim Treasury will be responsible.

There is a long and detailed discussion about public funds in the system of governments, and those public funds which are at the disposal of the just *imam* (leader). There is also a detailed discussion on the money which is submitted to qualified jurists and determining the priorities and limits of spending. My later father has addressed many aspects of such discussions in his book *al-Fiqh al-Dawlah* (The Law of Government) and *al-Iqtisaad* (The Economy), in addition to other books.

The Pyramid of Happiness: Piety, Health and Wealth

Imam Ali (a) says:

> Know that one of the blessings is to have abundant wealth, and what is better than abundant wealth is physical health, and what is better than physical health is the piety of the heart.[222]

Abundance of wealth is among the Divine blessings; but poverty is not, for it is a calamity. However, this *hadith* defines for us the pyramid of happiness, and at the top of the pyramid is the piety of the heart and abstaining from sins. A person who is truly happy is the pious individual. Then physical health comes next in the middle of the pyramid, and at the bottom of it comes the abundance of wealth, for it is quite evident that the one who is healthy but poor is happier and more blissful than the one who is not physically healthy (but is rich). For instance, he is more blissful than the one who suffers from a terminal illness such as cancer or AIDS, or even illnesses such as Alzheimer's or colonic diseases, even though that ill person may be wealthy. This means that no one would sacrifice their health for gaining wealth and accumulating money in one's bank account.

[222] *Ghurar al-Hikam*, vol. 1, p. 172, ch. 6, trad. 25.

Here are some goals or objectives for having wealth:

Imam Ali (a) narrates from Prophet Muhammad (s) that he said:

> Poverty is better for my nation than richness, except for the one who lifts a burden or gives in times of tragedy.[223]

Being rich is not inherently of value. It becomes valuable if it used for the right purpose. If one uses it to lift a burden, such as sponsoring orphans, widows and the needy, or even taking care of one's family costs, taking care of one's extended family, an organization or union, or even sponsoring the costs of the Marja' system, then such wealth is of value. In addition, wealth is of value if it is used during times of tragedy, such as giving humanitarian aid after an earthquake, hurricane or flood, or even after the waves of recession that strike the market, or elsewhere for a noble cause.

Protecting Honor or Chastity

Imam Ali (a) says in one of his sermons:

> The best of deeds is protecting honor or chastity with wealth"[224]

Making money is called for, not for the sake of just making money, but for the sake of accomplishing noble objectives such as protecting honor and chastity. Honor (*'irdh* in Arabic) is general and is not limited to personal honor. It also includes family honor, a nation's honor, a civilization's honor, and the honor of religion. This means that it is necessary to expend wealth to protect social honor and a healthy social reputation. Furthermore, spending money to protect honor generates economic returns, for a businessman who has a good reputation will gain the trust of the people by his honesty and good reputation. Others will deal with him and his wealth will increase.

---

[223] *Mustadrak al-Wasa'il*, vol. 12, p. 15, ch. 5, trad. 2.

[224] *Al-Kafi*, vol. 4, p. 49. Also refer to *Wasa'il al-Shia*, vol. 16, p. 192.

In a *hadith*, Imam Ali (a) says:

> Protect your honor with wealth.[225]

This is a command by the Imam, and a command means it is mandatory for us to follow it. Also, it seems that the honor that must be protected in this *hadith* is that which is mandatory to protect; otherwise, if it is not an honor that is mandatory to protect, then it is recommended to protect it.

Imam Ali (a) says:

> The best of your wealth is that which protects your honor.[226]

It is the best of wealth when we examine its essence, not its outside surface or appearance. It is also the best of wealth when we examine how it elevates the spirit, not the ostentation of materialism. Honor is the essence and the jewel, whereas wealth is the material, shape and appearance.

In another *hadith*, Imam Ali (a) says:

> You do not lose from your money that which is spent on protecting your honor.[227]

That is because wealth transforms into a higher value and becomes embodied in an elevated image, and because it also brings you more money as discussed earlier.

Imam Ali (a) also says:

> It is noble for a person to sacrifice themselves and protect their honor.[228]

The Definitions and Dimensions of "Honor"

"Honor" is a multi-dimensional notion that has multiple domains:

The First Domain: The specific meaning of honor, which refers

---

[225] *Ghurar al-Hikam*, vol. 1, p. 344, ch. 28, trad. 41.

[226] Ibid., vol. 1, p. 348, ch. 29, trad. 12.

[227] Ibid., vol. 2, p. 139, ch. 74, trad. 16.

[228] Ibid., vol. 2, p. 253, ch. 78, trad. 96.

to one's personal honor or family honor in its moral dimension.

The Second Domain: The general meaning of honor, which includes everything connected to social status, a good moral, financial, and administrative reputation. This general meaning also includes one's personal honor, family honor, and the honor of his party, extended family or tribe, alignment, country, and nation as well.

In the book *Majma' al-Bahrain*, the author says when defining the term "*irdh*" (honor):

> It is said that it is the object of praising or criticizing a human being, whether it is in himself, his ancestors, or those whose affairs are binding for him. It is also said that it is the aspect of a person, whether from himself or his family, which he protects and safeguards from being ridiculed or disgraced.

In the general outlook on wealth, wealth must serve a purpose, and among the most important purposes is protecting one's honor in both domains. Therefore, based on this, it is incumbent on individuals, families, groups, organizations, parties, countries, and nations to allocate a good amount of wealth to enjoy a good reputation and a wonderful status among all nations and in social domains, and to also avert or deflect all types of accusations, backbiting, and defamation.

Also, this serves to make individuals become known for being honest, trustworthy, sincere, righteous, pious, doing good deeds, qualified, competent, serious, striving, and having an athletic and consultative spirit. In addition to being known for such qualities, one must also strive to possess these qualities in reality.

In this regards, we have a statement from Prophet Abraham (a) in which he has said:

> And grant me an honorable reputation among the later generations.[229]

[229] Quran, Surah al-Shu'araa' (26) verse 84.

It is also necessary to protect one's most important honor with one's honor. Imam Ali (a) says:

> Venerate your honor with your own honor - be kind and gracious and you will be served, and have forbearance and you will advance forward.[230]

The narrations we have received from the Commander of the Faithful Imam Ali (a) point us to the reality that not protecting one's honor is ignoble and low. He says:

> It is ignobile for a man to protect his wealth but sacrifice or neglect his honor.[231]

In another *hadith*, the Imam (a) says:

> Having abundant wealth at the expense of losing honor is disgraceful.[232]

Honor is so important that Imam Ali (a), states:

> It is noble for a man to sacrifice himself but protect his honor.[233]

This means that a person should sacrifice one's life for the sake of protecting one's honor. From a religious standpoint, there are several examples for that. For instance, one must defend the honor of his family—his mother, wife, daughter or others—from being violated. Another example is defending the honor—the reputation—of Islam and Muslims from being polluted. In fact, honor is so important such that some jurists, among them my late father, have issued a verdict banning certain punishments in the Islamic Penal Code from being executed if it damages the image of Islam and Muslims.

The details of such a ruling can be found in my father's

[230] *Ghurar al-Hikam*, vol. 2, p. 305, ch. 83, trad. 51.

[231] Ibid., vol. 2, p. 253, ch. 78, trad. 97.

[232] Ibid., vol. 2, p. 301, ch. 83, trad. 9.

[233] Ibid., vol. 2, p. 253, ch. 78, trad. 96.

book *al-Fiqh: al-Dawlha al-Islamiyyah* (The Law of the Islamic Government).

In a *hadith*, Imam Ali (a) says:

> Protect your honor by expending your wealth.[234]

Spending Wealth in God's Obedience

Imam Ali (a) says:

> The greatest remorse on the Day of Judgment will be the remorse of an individual who made a living not in Allah's obedience, but then a person inherited him and spent that wealth in Allah's obedience, and so he [the second person] will enter Heaven because of it, while the first one will enter Hell because of it.[235]

Wealth is a bridge that connects this world to the Hereafter. A person is able to buy happiness in this world and paradise in the Hereafter with one's wealth, by making a lawful living and spending it appropriately. On the other hand, a person is able to buy wretchedness, enemies, and hatred in this world and Hell in the Hereafter with one's wealth by "making a living not in Allah's obedience..."

In another *hadith*, Imam Ali (a) says:

> A person is not given the sustenance (blessings) of wealth who does not spend it.[236]

Does wealth have an inherent value? No, and a thousand nos. What is the value of frozen money stored in boxes, buried in the earth, or kept in the bank? Money becomes valuable when you use it to bring happiness or bliss to your family, group and nation, and you use it to stimulate the economy. Allah the Almighty states:

---

[234] Ibid., vol. 2, p. 301, ch. 83, trad. 8.

[235] *Nahj al-Balagha*, maxim 429.

[236] *Ghurar al-Hikam*, vol. 2, p. 139, ch. 74, trad. 13.

> And those who amass gold and silver and do not spend them in the way of Allah, announce to them the tidings of a painful chastisement.[237]

Therefore, it is for this reason that the Imam (a) says:

> A person is not given the sustenance of wealth who does not spend it.

for the one who does not spend wealth on education, healthcare, security, advancement and progress for oneself, family and society is essentially deprived from wealth.

Happiness in this World and Success in the Hereafter

It has been narrated that the Commander of the Faithful Imam Ali (a) said:

> O son of Adam, let not your greatest concern be a day which you might not live to see, and for each day that you live, God will deliver to you your sustenance; and know that whatever you make above what you need you are amassing it for someone else. You work so hard for it in this life but you delight your inheritor with it, and on top of that, your accountability for it will be long on the Day of Judgment. Therefore, let your wealth bring you happiness in your life, and offer for your hereafter a provision that will be ahead of you, for the journey is very far, the appointment is the Day of Judgment, and the destination is either Heaven or Hell.[238]

Wealth itself is not a goal, but it is a means only, and the goal is two:

1. To be happy and blissful in your life ("let your wealth bring you happiness in your life"). The essence of happiness is to please your Lord with your money, and also to please your

---

[237] *Quran*, Surah al-Tawbah (9) verse 34.

[238] *Mustadrak al-Wasa'il*, vol. 13, p. 35, ch. 11, hadith no. 7.

family, neighbors, community, and nation with your money by offering it to them, spending it on them, gifting them presents, donations and charitable contributions—all of which will make you reach to the peak of humanity. Having done that, you will also satisfy your own conscience.

2. To prepare and develop your afterlife with your money, for it is your abode and place of final settlement. As we have seen, these two goals are interlinked with a solid link, and in fact, they are two sides of the same coin.

Poverty is Damaging

Imam Ali (a) says:

> Poverty silences the clever and intelligent one from his arguments or proofs, and the poor person is a stranger even in his homeland."

Why does poverty silence the shrewd and intelligent one from his arguments and proofs? The answer is that a poor person does not own the means and channels to defend his arguments, support them, propagate them and persuade others by them. Does poverty allow the poor to own newspapers, magazines, radio and television channels? Is it in the capacity of the poor to establish schools and educational institutions which graduate scholars or academics who carry their ideology, defend it with proofs, and deliver it to others? Therefore, the poor must strive to become wealthy if they want to have an ideology, message, and goal in life.

As for the Imam's (a) statement that "the poor is a stranger even in his homeland," it is because the one who lacks wealth, tools, instruments and infrastructure institutions, people will not pay any attention to him, for why should they pay attention to him. Therefore, he will usually be a stranger in his own hometown; so do not stay or become poor or else you will become a stranger.

The Poorest Person

Imam Ali (a) says:

> The poorest person is the one who is very cheap with himself even though he is rich and wealthy, and then he bequeaths his wealth to others.[239]

Isn't poverty but deprivation? Which poor person is poorer than the one who is wealthy but deprived? Which poor is poorer than the one who amasses money for others, but deprives himself even though he has desperate needs?

The Culture of "Master" not "Captive"

Imam Ali (a) says:

> Do not need anyone—by needing only Allah—and you shall be his counterpart; be in need to whomever you want and you shall be his captive; and do a favor to whomever you want and you shall be his master.[240]

People fall under three categories:

1. The "master," and he is the one who does good to others and bestows them with his favors.
2. The "captive," and he is the one who stretches his hand to other people.
3. The "counterpart," and he is the who neither does good to people nor does he ask anything from them.

Which of these categories is the best, and of which of them do you want to be?

If the culture of being a "master" and doing good spreads in society, most poor people will become rich who do good instead of being poor captives. Furthermore, if this culture becomes widespread, society will be much more productive. Instead of having the poor stay accustomed to living on charity, donations, and social or government contributions, they could transform

[239] *Ghurar al-Hikam*, vol. 1, p. 209, ch. 8, p. 517.

[240] *Kanz al-Fawa'id*, vol. 2, p. 194.

into businessmen, innovative farmers and skilled workers. Would not the overall state of the economy be more powerful, solid, and stable?

There may always be a class of people who can never cross the poverty line, due to a disability or other factors, and in this case, others must fulfill their responsibility by doing good to them. As Allah states:

> Surely Allah enjoins justice and kindness.[241]

The Five Pillars

It has been narrated that when Imam Ali (a) would come back from a *jihad* (war), he would dedicate his time to educate people and give them their rights (by being a judge). When he would finish that, he would go work to on a garden that he was developing with his own hands, and he would mention God's name when he would work.[242] What we take from this *hadith* is that the following five pillars are fundamental and necessary, as Imam Ali (a) gave them time and priority:

1. The struggle *(jihad)* in the way of Allah;
2. Teaching and educating people;
3. Judging people and ending their disputes;
4. Working with one's hands;
5. Remembering and mentioning Allah while working.

The One Who Works in this World is a Winner in the Hereafter

It has been narrated that Prophet Muhammad (s) said:

> The one who eats (makes a living) from the work of his hands will pass the *siraat* (the bridge to Heaven) like a

[241] *Quran*, Surah an-Nahl (16) verse 90,

[242] *Mustadrak al-Wasa'il*, vol. 13, p. 25. Also refer to *Irshaad al-Qulub*, vol. 2, p. 218.

> flash of lightning.[243]

It is possible that one of the reasons a person will have such a successful outcome is that the one who works hard, strives, and exerts the effort in this life to make a lawful living instead of being a burden on others will be compensated in the Hereafter by quickly passing the *siraat* and being saved from its dangers. Consequently, he will reach Heaven, which is the ultimate destination and success, as fast as possible.

The One Who Works is Better than the Disciples of Prophet Jesus (a)

It has been narrated that the disciples would follow Prophet Jesus (a), and when they would become hungry they would say to him:

> O Spriit of God (a title of Jesus), we have become hungry! Then he would strike his hand on the ground, whether it was a flat land or a mountain, and two loaves of bread would come out for each of the disciples to eat. When they would become thirsty, they would say: O Spirit of God, we have become thirsty! Then he would strike his hand on the ground, whether it was a flat land or a mountain, and water would flow for them to drink. Then they said to him: O Spirit of God, who is better than us? Whenever we desire, you feed us, and whenever we desire, you quench our thirst, and we have believed in you and followed you. He said to them: Better than you is the one who works with his hands and then eats from his work. After that, they started to wash clothes for a wage.[244]

This means that working and depending on one's own self in fulfilling one's personal needs is better than depending on others

243 *Jame' al-Akhbar*, p. 139, ch. 99. Also refer to *Mustadrak al-Wasa'il*, vol. 13, pp. 23-24, hadith no. 5.

244 *Majma' al-Bayan*, vol. 1, p. 448. Also refer to *Mustadrak al-Wasa'il*, vol. 13, p. 33, ch. 8, trad. 2.

even if that person is a prophet, and even if the food he is giving is divine and miraculous. This sends a message to all of those who abandon serious or arduous work and try to compensate for that (lack of work) by resorting to supplicating and beseeching God only.

One *hadith* states:

> Work, then rely on God.[245]

Even Prophets Were Required to Work

It has been narrated that Imam al-Sadiq (a) quoted Imam Ali (a) saying:

> Allah the Almighty revealed to Prophet David (a): You are such a good slave—except that you eat from public funds and you do not work with your hands. David (a) cried forty days,[246] so Allah revealed to the iron: Be softened for my servant David. Allah softened iron for him, so he would make one armor per day and sell it for one thousand *dirhams* (silver coins). He made three-hundred and sixty armors, selling them for three-hundred and sixty thousand *dirhams*, thereby not needing public funds.[247]

This means that even prophets, who are at the peak of humanity and are responsible for delivering the message and guiding people, have to work to secure a living instead of relying on public funds. One of the reasons behind this could be that the prophets are role models for people to follow. However, this does not mean that we should not have people specialized in

---

[245] *Meshkat al-Anwar*, p. 551.

[246] It seems that there were no work opportunities for David (a), or he was unaware of them, or unaware of what his role would exactly be. Thus, he cried out of fear of God and to earn God's compassion so then He showed him a type of work that would please Him.

[247] *Al-Kafi*, vol. 5, p. 73, trad. 5.

certain professions such as teaching or preaching, or those who are not able to innovate or fulfill their responsibilities without depending on public funds or government money.

Working with One's Hands is the Way of the Prophets

Hasan son of Ali son of Abi Hamza narrates from his father saying:

> I saw Abal Hasan (a) (Imam al-Kadhim) working in a field of his and his feet were soaked in sweat. So I asked him, 'May my life be sacrificed for you, where are the men (workers)?' He said: 'O Ali, the one who is better than me and my father worked with his hands in his land.' I asked him, 'Who is that?' He said, 'The Messenger of Allah (a), the Commander of the Faithful (a), and all of my forefathers (peace be upon them) worked with their hands, and doing so is the way of the prophets, messengers, and righteous servants.'[248]

The Imam explained to us that working is the way of the prophets, messengers and righteous servants of God. Therefore, the Imam working wasn't an isolated incident or unique event. Work that involves weariness or hard labor has many benefits and effects such as:

1. Achieving self-sufficiency in one's personal life.
2. A nation achieves self-sufficiency if all of the people get accustomed to productive work.
3. Physical health and well-being, and thus we find that villagers and workers (who do physical labor) are stronger, physically fitter, and heathier than those who are inactive, work in offices, or perform routine duties.
4. Purifying the body from germs, microbes and toxins through perspiration.

---

[248] *Man La Yahdharah al-Faqih*, vol. 3, p. 98, trad. 28.

5. Polishing the personality of a human being, as working makes one accustomed to producing and keeps one away from dependence on others.
6. Grants the human being a mark of humbleness, and it also strengthens one's connection to nature.
7. It grants the human being forbearance, perseverance, patience, and strength to face challenges and tragedies.
8. Increases the human being's dignity, honor, and status, and it gives a person greater credibility.

Among the Signs of Treacherous Times: Evildoers Rise and Businessmen Become Stingy

Imam Ali (a) said:

> A biting time will come upon people in which the rich will seize their possessions with their tooth (become stingy) although not commanded to do so. Allah the Glorified states: 'And forget not generosity among yourselves.'[249] The wicked will rise up, while the virtuous will remain low, and purchases will be made from the helpless, although the Messenger of Allah (s) prohibited purchasing from the helpless.[250]

We understand the following from this *hadith*:

1. Do not seize your possessions with your teeth and be stingy. Instead, be generous, giving and charitable.
2. Do not allow the wicked to rise and take charge, and prevent them from running the economy. If they take charge and be at the top, they will be just as Imam Ali (a) described: They swallow up Allah's wealth like a camel devours the foliage of spring.[251]

---

[249] *Quran*, Surah al-Baqarah (2) verse 237.

[250] *Nahj al-Balagha*, maxim 468.

[251] Ibid., sermon 3.

3. Do not degrade the righteous and virtuous, do not humiliate them, and do not belittle them with words, actions, or stance. Do not allow anyone to do that either.
4. Do not take advantage of people's difficult circumstances by buying their house, business, or goods for a cheap price.

A Balanced View of Workers and Work

Imam Ali (a) says:

> The sustenance that has been determined for you (by God) will not elude you or slip away from you, so be brief in your pursuit (to make a living).[252]

Another *hadith* states:

> Sustenance is of two types: one that you pursue and one that pursues you.

What is meant by the expression: "the sustenance that has been determined for you will not slip away from you" in the above mentioned *hadith*? What is meant by the expression "sustenance is not achieved by avarice and vying" in a *hadith* which will follow? What is meant by the expression "his pursuit will not increase that which has been determined for him?" What is meant by all of these is what is stated in the above mentioned *hadith* which says: "and one that pursues you," meaning that which is determined in the preserved tablet.[253]

Therefore, these *ahadith* offer us a comprehensive outlook on the issue of sustenance - as they do not ignore making a living altogether, and at the same time they discourage from being too avaricious and desperate to make money. Instead, one should "be brief in your pursuit," meaning pursue making a living, but do so with wisdom, moderation and brevity. Our pursuit and attempt should not be too aggressive and excessive.

---

[252] *Ghurar al-Hikam*, vol. 2, p. 130, ch. 72, trad. 37.

[253] The preserved tablet (*lawh al-mahfoodh*) is a reference to the fixed decrees of God.

As for the sustenance which we pursue, it falls in the domain of the contingent tablet, which is framed and limited by the preserved tablet. Therefore, there is room to move and maneuver, and the movement can be significant, but there are limits to this movement (pursuit). So pursue sustenance, but do so from lawful sources, and spend, but do so appropriately.[254]

Wealth and Blessings can Transform into a Curse

Imam Ali (a) says:

> Know with full conviction that Allah has not fixed for any person more livelihood than what has been ordained in the Book of Destiny, even though one's means (of seeking it) may be great, one's craving for it intense and the efforts for it acute; nor does the weakness of a person or the paucity of one's means stand in the way between what is ordained in the Book of Destiny and oneself. A person who realizes this and acts upon it is the best of them all in terms of comfort and benefit, while one who disregards it and doubts it exceeds all people in disadvantages. Very often a favored person is being slowly driven (towards punishment) through those favors; and very often an afflicted person is being done good through one's affliction. Therefore, O listener, increase your gratefulness, lessen your haste and stay within the bounds of your livelihood.[255]

The entire *hadith* is fascinating, but we will stop at the phrase "very often a favored person is being slowly driven (towards punishment) through these favors" and say the following: Wealth, beauty, fame, and power are all favors or blessings, but what is important is the end since all of these favors can become

[254] For instance, one should not give money to corrupt or deviant organizations, nor should one spend on supporting injustice, gambling, or moral corruption such as prostitution in any way.

[255] *Nahj al-Balagha*, maxim 273.

a curse.

As the Imam (a) states:

> Very often a favored person is being slowly driven (towards punishment) through those favors."

Sometimes one's wealth can push him towards oppressing others, violating the rights of others, arrogance, and despotism. Allah the Almighty states:

> Nay, surely the human being transgresses, when he believes himself to be self-sufficient (or wealthy).[256]

In another verse, He states:

> Let not the unbelievers imagine that the respite We grant them is good for them. We grant them respite so that they may grow in wickedness.[257]

The Second Point

Obligations and Responsibilities of the Poor

Does a poor person have to surrender to his poverty? Is a poor person even capable of surrendering to his poverty? Or are there religious and rational obligations upon him, which if he fulfills, he is guaranteed to exit the poverty line in the long run? Does a poor person have responsibilities which determine how he should deal with himself and others as long as he lives the life of poverty and deprivation? This is what we will briefly discuss in this section.

You Must be Self-Sufficient

Imam Ali (a) says:

> Whoever opens a door of asking (begging) on himself,

---

256 *Quran*, Surah al-Alaq (96) verses 6-7.

257 *Quran*, Surah Aal Imran (3) verse 178.

> Allah will open a door of poverty for him.[258]

This means that one should not ask and beg, but instead work and work harder. This is among the most important obligations of the poor, and we have discussed this in another part of the book.

Protect Yourself from that which is Prohibited

Imam Ali (a) says:

> Being chaste/virtuous is the adornment of the poor, and being thankful is the adornment of the rich.[259]

Being chaste or virtuous means that one abstains from everything prohibited - from theft, deception, cheating, begging, humiliating oneself, and this abstinence is the adornment of the poor, and it is among the most important features of the deprived.

Conceal Your Agony

Imam Ali (a) says:

> A person who reveals his agony to other people has exposed himself.[260]

Agony (*dharr* in Arabic) is a general term that includes diseases, disputes, enmities, inadequacies, and poverty. A person who suffers an affliction should protect their dignity by not revealing it to this and that person, or telling others about his weaknesses and problems. One should not evoke their pity or beg for money. Instead, one should strive to solve one's problems, treat afflictions wisely, work hard, be patient, and persevere in order to achieve progress and completion.

Do Not Ask

Imam Ali (a) says:

---

[258] *Kanz al-Fawa'id*, vol. 2, p. 193.

[259] Ibid.

[260] Ibid., vol. 2, p. 194.

> The best richness is to avoid asking.

Asking is like getting a fish, and then you will go back needy. If you avoid asking however, and instead indulge in working, then you will get a fishing net which will generate resources for you.

Avoid Abasing Yourself

Imam Ali (a) says:

> The worst poverty is habitually abasing yourself.

Abasing or humbling yourself (for the sake of getting money) is humiliation, and it is a type of psychological poverty which brings about material poverty. Worse than that is if it becomes a fixed habit, and this is what the Imam (a) referred to by saying "habitually abasing yourself."

Be Content

Imam Ali (a) says:

> There is no possession which eradicates poverty like being satisfied and content.[261]

Being content is the key to success, and is there a fortune greater than the fortune of happiness? Therefore, contentment is the greatest possession. It is important to note that one's needs do not go with the abundance of wealth. In fact, the abundance of wealth makes one's needs more deeply rooted and makes the rich attached to money with the ropes of avarice. Being satisfied however, is a psychological and spiritual richness which protects one from being in need of materialism. This does not mean that one neglects making money or avoids becoming wealthy; it simply means that one should not be held captive to money and be enslaved to wealth. Instead, be the master and the ruler. Possess wealth but then spend it on charitable or good causes. In addition, be content with what you have, and do not pursue more by resorting to unlawful means.

---

[261] Ibid.

Decipher between being Wasteful and being Economical

The Commander of the Faithful Imam Ali (a) says:

> Anything which exceeds being economical is wasteful.[262]

This is a general rule and clear standard, for sometimes antithetical qualities can be defined by their antithesis due to the latter's clarity, or because the former does not have something like it to be defined by, or one keeps having a constant doubt about it.[263]

The word "*iqtisaad*" in Arabic (which the Imam uses in the *hadith* and is translated as being economical) comes from the root word "*qasd*," which means to be moderate and not fall to either extremes, which is squandering or being stingy.

My late father used to say: "Being economical is sometimes determined by quantity and sometimes by quality, and sometimes applies to materialistic matters and sometime to spiritual matters."[264]

Imam Ali (a) says:

> Anything which exceeds your needs is wasteful.[265]

For example, if you have two homes and one is enough for you, then that is wasteful; and if you have two cars and one car is sufficient for you, then that is wasteful too.

It is from the wisdom of Imam Ali (a) that he has worded this standard (of being economical) using various expressions so that

---

[262] *Ghurar al-Hikam*, vol. 2, p. 85, ch. 62, trad. 73.

[263] For example, the notion of being economical is easier to understand than the notion of being wasteful because it is not that clear what constitutes wastefulness or squandering. Thus, the Imam (a) in the hadith defines wastefulness as anything which exceeds being economical.

[264] *Al-Fiqh: al-Iqtisaad* (The Law of Economics), vol. 107 of the *Fiqh Encyclopedia*, pp. 7-8.

[265] *Ghurar al-Hikam*, vol. 2, p. 259, ch. 79, trad. 13.

each expression has an impact on or guides certain groups of people.

Work for the Interest of the Family

It has been narrated that Imam Ali (a) said:

> A person who sets out early morning in the way of Allah is not greater than the person who sets our early in the morning to seek for his children and family what benefits them (or improves their livelihood).[266]

These are two wings that ensure a healthy society, the wing of struggle (*jihad*) and the wing of self-sufficiency and improving the livelihood of one's family.

Strive but without Avarice or Greed

It has been narrated that Imam Ali (a) said:

> I am amazed at a person who knows that Allah has fixed and guaranteed the sustenance (of people) and that his pursuit will not increase that which has been preordained for him, yet he is avaricious and excessively pursuant in seeking (more) sustenance.[267]

Striving or pursuing to make a living is only one of the factors which brings about sustenance, and all power belongs to Allah before and after. Allah has instructed us to seek sustenance, but not excessively and greedily. One should seek sustenance with moderation and without any avarice which may lead one to indulge in unlawful acts that will cause people's rights to be violated.

It has been narrated that Imam Ali (a) said:

> Be brief in seeking sustenance, for how many greedy people are unsuccessful, while a moderate person does

[266] *Da'a'em al-Islam*, vol. 2, p. 15, ch. 1, trad. 9.

[267] *Ghurar al-Hikam*, vol. 2, p. 38, ch. 54, trad. 31.

> not fail.[268]

It seems that this *hadith*, which instructs one to be brief in seeking sustenance, is simply advising us that the one who is brief in seeking sustenance will not fail.[269] We say that this command to be brief in seeking sustenance is simply an advice in the form of a command not because the Imam (a) states the reason or rationale behind the command, as some have stated,[270] but because the average person understands from this *hadith*, in addition to the consensus of scholars, that avarice by itself is not prohibited (*haram* and sinful) if it does not lead to prohibited acts.[271] In any case, the rationale that the Imam (a) states suffices to encourage people to be brief in seeking sustenance.

It has also been narrated that Imam Ali (a) said:

> Humble yourself with obedience (to God), embellish it with contentment, and be brief in seeking sustenance and making a living.[272]

The essence of the *hadith* is:

1. The importance of obedience of the Almighty God within the

---

[268] Ibid., vol. 1, p. 149, ch. 3, trad. 61.

[269] Such commands in Islamic Jurisprudence are called "*awamir irshadiyya*," meaning that they are not religious directives which if not observed one is deemed sinful and will be punished. They are simply commands which give us advice. To the contrary, religious commands are called "*awamir wawlawiyya*." If such commands are obligatory, then not observing them is a sin.

[270] Some have stated that whenever a *hadith* specifies the rationale behind its command, the command becomes an advisory command which simply directs us to what is good or bad, not a religious command. For further details, refer to the book "*al-Awamer al-Mawlawiyya wal Irshadiyya*" by the author.

[271] If the command to avoid avarice was a "*mawlawi*" command, meaning a religiously binding command, then it would be prohibited even if it did not lead to any prohibited acts.

[272] *Ghurar al-Hikam*, vol. 1, p. 366, ch. 32, trad. 40.

framework of one's relationship with the Creator.

2. Being content with one's living standards, not with one's good deeds, within the framework of one's needs. What indicates this or the path to achieve this is being brief in seeking sustenance and being moderate in making a living.

Decrease Your Desire/Yearning and be Brief in Seeking Sustenance

Imam Ali (a) states:

> Six things test the religion of a person: the strength of their religion, the truthfulness of their certainty, the scope of their piety, opposition to their desires, lowering their desires or yearnings, and being brief in seeking sustenance.[273]

The word "religion" in this *hadith* has multiple meanings, and some meanings are more general than others. According to some meanings of religion, if one lacks religion, then one is no longer a Muslim; while according to others, if one lacks religion, one is still considered to be a Muslim. Some meanings also point to what is obligatory, some to what is recommended, and some to what is considered completion or perfection.[274]

This *hadith* refers to the second meaning of religion (meaning that if one lacks those six), one is still considered a Muslim, or they are recommended and part of completion) because the Imam (a) says that these six things test one's faith, and then he mentions decreasing one's desires and being brief in seeking sustenance, both of which indicate reliance on God from one aspect (the more general meaning of religion) and making a lawful living from another aspect (the more specific meaning of religion). As for reducing one's desires, it could mean avoiding that which is

[273] Ibid., vol. 1, p. 397, ch. 39, trad. 82.

[274] For further details, refer to the book *Fiqh al-Ijtihaad wal Taqleed* by the author.

prohibited, or it could mean avoiding excessive desires, due to greed and avarice for worldly matters.

Deal with what has Come to and what has Not Come to You Wisely

Imam Ali (a) states:

> Take from this world what has come to you, and turn away from what has turned away from you, but if you do not do that, then be moderate in seeking sustenance.[275]

It seems that the Imam (a) is referring to the threefold division when it comes to dealing with money, wealth and other matters. It is as follows:

1. What comes to you from the world (the favors or bounties of this world), take it and do not avoid it like monks or dervishes do.
2. Turn away from what turned away from you; and do not indulge - especially in prohibited acts - to reach that which turned away from you.
3. As for what does not naturally come to you except with effort, and what turns away from you naturally but you can reach it with effort, then seek it, but do so moderately and briefly without greed or avarice.

Seek Your Fortune - but Moderately

Imam Ali (a) states:

> The world circulates, so seek your fortune from it moderately.[276]

If the world revolves, circulates, changes and shifts from one person to another, then one should be moderate or brief in seeking sustenance. When good opportunities present themselves, one

---

[275] *Nahj al-Balagha*, maxim 393.

[276] *Kanz al-Fawa'id*, vol. 1, p. 61. Also refer to *A'alaam al-Deen*, p. 173.

should take advantage of them, and one should avoid seeking to board a train which has passed or ride a horse which has expired.

Make Your Income Pure

It has been reported that Imam Ali (a) said:

> The Messenger of Allah (s) said, 'Whoever wants to have his prayers answered should make his income pure.'[277]

Purifying one's income is a general notion that indicates two types of making a living:

1. Making a living from legitimate[278] sources and avoiding that which is prohibited.
2. Making a living from known[279] sources and avoiding doubtful or suspicious sources.

If a person purifies their income from these two aspects, then one's prayers will be answered for a number of reasons. One of them is that one will resist against temptations, and that carries a reward. Another is that if one purifies their income, then their soul, self and body will also become purified. Thus, one's prayers will be answered.

Adorn Yourself with Gracious Patience

It has been reported that Prophet Muhammad (s) said to Imam Ali (a) in the *hadith* of prohibitions:

> A person who is not content with the sustenance that Allah has decreed for him, or complains, or is not patient and content, then a single good deed will not be accepted from him, and he will meet Allah while He is angry at

[277] *Mustadrak al-Wasa'il*, vol. 13, p. 27, ch. 10, trad. 2, p. 224.

[278] They are legitimate either by a solid proof (such as a *hadith*) or by a principle (in the science of jurisprudence). For instance, one principle says: "Everything is lawful to you except that which is known to be prohibited."

[279] Sources which have a solid proof for their lawfulness.

> him, unless he repents.[280]

There are two types of patience, positive patience and negative patience. Positive patience means endurance and forbearance without any clamor or complaints. It means facing dangers and tragedies with a strong and stable spirit and controlling one's anxiety. Negative patience means to stagnate, be idle, surrender, and not make any effort to change your condition within religious and rational limits. This type of patience is unacceptable. Based on that, the poor and those with limited income should adorn themselves with positive, active patience, and avoid negative patience that kills.

Do not Have Negative Thoughts about God, Do not Deny the Rights, and Do not be Stingy

Imam Ali (a) says:

> Among the pieces of advice that Luqman gave to his son was this: 'O my son, the one who has weak faith and is tired of seeking sustenance should learn a lesson from the fact that Allah created him in three conditions and he delivered to him his sustenance without him seeking it or trying to obtain it. He should learn a lesson from that and know that Allah will deliver his sustenance in the fourth condition too. As for the first condition, it is when one was in the womb of their mother and God would deliver to him his sustenance in that secure repository. No heat or cold harms the fetus. Then God took him out of there and caused the milk of his mother to flow, giving him nourishment without having to make any effort. Then he weaned him from that and delivered to him his sustenance from the work of his parents, with compassion and mercy. Then when one grows up and matures, and he starts to make a living for himself, he

[280] *Man La Yahdharoh al-Faqih*, vol. 4, p. 7, ch. 1, trad. 1.

> feels as if he has no way out, and he begins to see his Lord negatively, he denies the rights of others in his money, and he becomes stingy with himself and his family for fear of becoming poor.[281]

The past is the mirror to the future, at the individual and national level. If Allah the Almighty Creator has taken care of your entire past, as this *hadith* explains, then why should you have negative thoughts about your Lord when it comes to your future? Why do you deny the rights of Allah, which he has placed in your wealth, when you only have to give some of what He has given you? Why do you become stingy with yourself and your family? Is it not because of your weak faith and your ignorance about the reality of this world? Therefore:

1. Do not ever have negative thoughts about your Lord.
2. Never deny the rights imposed upon you in regards to your wealth (such as *khums*, *zakat*, and other obligatory spendings on your family and others).
3. Do not ever be stingy with yourself and your family for fear of becoming poor, and never accumulate your wealth by making your bank accounts bigger and bigger day after day, while you and your family live deprived from the goodly blessings that Allah has endowed you with. Is this not like the one who stores his car in the garage and does not use it for fear of his car breaking down or becoming used?

Seek Sustenance through Legitimate and Legal Channels

It has been narrated that Imam Ali (a) said in his will to his son Muhammad ibn al-Hanafiyya:

> O my son, never rely on baseless wishes...O my son, there are two types of sustenance. One is a sustenance that you seek, and one is a sustenance that seeks you, and even if

[281] *Bihar al-Anwar*, vol. 100, p. 30, ch. 2, trad. 54.

> you do not go to it, it will come to you. Therefore, do not add to your daily concern the concern for your whole year. It suffices you to be concerned about the day you are in. If it has been decreed for you to live the following year, then Allah the Almighty will deliver to you a new sustenance every morning, and if the upcoming year is not a part of your life, then what is the point of being concerned about and distressed over something which is not yours? Know that no seeker will beat you to your sustenance, and no one will overcome you, and what has been decreed for you will not be kept away from you. How many a seeker have you seen who exhausts himself, but his sustenance is tightfisted with him? How many a moderate seeker have you seen who is aided by the decrees of Allah? Everyone will perish, and today is yours, but you are not certain that you will live to see tomorrow.[282]

This *hadith* overflows with wisdom and advice. Based on the wisdom contained in this *hadith*, it is incumbent on the human being to:

1. Seek sustenance within the framework of Islamic law if the person is religious, and within the framework of the natural (*fitrah*, or intrinsic), rational and humane laws.
2. Adorn himself with serenity, tranquility, composure, and equanimity if a misfortune affects one's wealth, or suddenly an adversity puts an end to years of one's efforts, work, and actions.

There are many lessons and pieces of wisdom in this will by Imam Ali (a). They are invaluable and require writing a separate paper to address them. Therefore, let us do justice to these luminous words by pondering over them and contemplating upon them, and by transforming them into a lamp that illuminates the path

[282] *Man La Yahdharoh al-Faqih*, vol. 4, p. 275, ch. 176, trad. 10.

for us throughout our lives.

Third Point

Ways and Tools to become Rich through Legitimate Means and to Exit Poverty

Does the religion of Islam and specifically the teachings of Imam Ali (a) have instructions that illuminate the path for the poor and teach them the ways and methods to exit the poverty line and show them effective ways to become rich through legitimate means? This is the point around which this section will revolve around briefly.

Knock on Different Doors, be Creative and take Calculated Risks

It has been reported that Imam al-Sadiq (a) narrated from his father, from his grandfather, from Imam Ali (a) that he said:

> Be more expectant for what you do not expect than what you expect, for Moses son of Amram (a) set out to find fire for his family, but Allah the Almighty spoke to him and he returned as a prophet. The Queen of Saba' (Bathsheba) departed (her kingdom) but ended up submitting (to Allah) with Solomon (a). The sorcerers of the Pharaoh set out to achieve glory for him but they returned as believers.[283]

Creative and innovative thinking along with taking calculated risks are considered among the most important ways to discover new methods of becoming rich. They are also considered among the most important ways for overcoming unexpected hurdles that company and business owners face. The essence of these two factors goes back to what the *hadith* refers to: "Be more expectant for what you do not expect than what you expect." This is because often times becoming rich, achieving relief and

---

[283] *Man La Yahdharah al-Faqih*, vol. 4, p. 284, ch. 176, trad. 30.

progressing in life come in unexpected ways, and in ways that you do not even think were possible.

Therefore, do not be conventional and stagnant, but instead be liberated and progressive. What we mean by conventional is one who continually lives captive to old and known methods; and what me mean by being liberated and progressive is one who liberates himself from the bondage of narrow and old ways. We do not mean breaking free from rational and religious principles, as is evident. Addressing this point comprehensively requires a separate book.

Do not take Uncalculated Risks

Imam Ali (a) says:

> Do not put yourself at risk with anything in expectation for more than that.[284]

Among the paths to failure is taking uncalculated risks. As for calculated risks, it is desired, and thus Imam Ali (a) says:

> The cowardly businessman is deprived, while the audacious businessman is given sustenance.[285]

A risk is considered to be uncalculated if it is not based on a comprehensive study of the market, the circumstances or dynamics of consumers, and the characteristics of those whom you deal with. One must also seek thorough consultation, healthy planning, wisely choose whom to work with and what methods or mechanisms to adopt, and constantly monitor and evaluate performance.

Maintain Your Wealth

Imam Ali (a) said in his will to his son Imam al-Hasan (a):

> Maintaining what is in your hands is more beloved to me

[284] *Nahj al-Balagha*, letter 31 which he wrote to his son Imam Hasan (a) after departing the Battle of Siffeen.

[285] *Mustadrak al-Wasa'il*, vol. 13, p. 294, Alulbayt edition, 1408 AH.

> than seeking what is in the hands of others.[286]

There are factors for the creation of wealth and richness, and there are factors for the preservation of wealth and richness. Just as a poor person must strive to create factors for the creation of wealth, the middle class and the rich must strive to maintain their wealth and richness.

Thus, Imam Ali (a) said:

> Maintaining what is in your hands...

What is in the hands of a person includes the company he inherited from his father, or the company that he founded, it also includes the factory that he built, bought or inherited. It even includes the farm or house which one owns, by maintaining them and protecting them from deterioration and damage. Otherwise, one will have to stretch one's hand to others, begging them for assistance!

Be Lenient in Your Livelihood

It has been narrated that Imam Ali (a) quoted the Messenger of Allah as having said:

> If Allah wants goodness for a household, then He will grant them understanding in religion, leniency in their livelihood, moderation (or economization) in their affairs, and He will dignify (or give respect to) their youngsters and their elders. But if Allah does not want goodness for them, then He will leave them neglected.[287]

Being lenient or gentle in one's livelihood is among the most important ways to make money, and it is also among the most important ways to maintain wealth and develop it. Leniency is the opposite of violence or harshness, and it means to have a calm, pleasant, and gentle nature.

---

[286] *Nahj al-Balagha*, letter 31.

[287] *Jame' Ahadith al-Shia*, vol. 17, p. 107, ch. 20, trad. 8, narrating from *al-Ja'fariyaat*, p. 149.

One *hadith* states that leniency is half of living. Leniency also means to work properly and do something well, as the book *Majma' al-Bahrain* states. It is evident that a person who is harsh and does not do one's work well will lose the trust of the people and will lose clients. As for the gentle, lenient people who does one's work well, whether that work is sewing, trading, or any other type of occupation or profession, his ties with people will expand and his good reputation will grant him greater credibility. People will flock to him, and he will move from one profit to another, and from one production to another.

Understanding religion will allow a person to avoid that which angers Allah and makes one disobey Allah, and so one will not cheat, take bribes, hoard, play with the measure, steal, embezzle, deceive, and so on. By not doing so, one will achieve Allah's satisfaction and gain the trust of the people, and so they will go to that person, and one's wealth will consequently increase.

Be Frugal in Your Life

It has been narrated that Imam Ali (a) said:

> Being frugal increases that which is meager.

Being frugal or economic requires knowledge, wisdom, expertise, and a strong will. Then, that which is little or meager will become abundant, and that which is abundant will become even more abundant. Being economical means to take a middle path between being wasteful and being stingy. One should not fall on either of the two extremes.

As it is evident, being wasteful is a cause for the destruction of wealth; and as for being stingy, even if it seems for some to be an ideal method to accumulate money and increase wealth, in reality it does the exact opposite because being stingy causes the following:

1. It ruins one's physical health.
2. It creates stress and ruins one's psychological health.

3. It makes people turn away from the stingy person, and thus one will lose or miss out on very important friendships which play a crucial role in the development of one's wealth. People simply avoid dealing with a stingy, greedy and avaricious person.

Imam Ali (a) says:

> Being economical will increase that which is little.[288]

The philosophy behind this is that wealth, just like any other power, accumulates just like drops accumulate. Just as streams form from raindrops, rivers form from streams, and then the oceans expand from rivers flowing into them and raindrops pouring on them, wealth accumulates and expands.

Imam Ali (a) says:

> Whoever holds on to frugality, richness will accompany him, and frugality will repair his poverty and defects.[289]

In another *hadith*, Imam Ali (a) says:

> Being economical [covers] half of one's expenses.[290]

The word "expenses" here refers to life expenses in general and financial obligations towards oneself, wife, children, family, friends and others. It is quite evident that a person who is not economical in one's food, clothing, transportation, cosmetics, leisure activities, and other luxuries, will impose a heavy burden on one's budget.

Being economical, however, by itself provides for one-half of life expenses, and thus Imam Ali (a) says:

> A person who is economical will not perish.[291]

In another *hadith*, he states:

---

[288] *Ghurar al-Hikam*, vol. 1, p. 30, ch. 1, trad. 567.

[289] Ibid., vol. 2, p. 241, ch. 77, trad. 1512.

[290] Ibid., vol. 1, p. 32, ch, 1, trad. 615.

[291] Ibid., vol 2, p. 131, ch. 72, trad. 44.

> A persons's expenses will be lighter if one is economical.[292]

This rule of thumb applies to individuals, organizations, parties, tribes, large families, nations and countries. All of them are capable of being economical and taking a moderate path in spending. At the same time, all of them are capable of squandering wealth and being wasteful, spending excessively without any measure and not based on any solid economic plan. The result is that the first (those who are economical) will be saved, while the second will perish.

You Must Always be Economical

Imam Ali (a) says:

> A person who is moderate in richness or in poverty has prepared oneself for the tragedies of life.[293]

Many of us are economical in times of poverty, but in times of richness we become wasteful and extravagant. This is a grave mistake because not being economical will bring about poverty. If frugality and moderation become the norm among the poor and the rich, then people will be safe from the calamities and tragedies of life or unexpected events, such as a sudden illness or an unexpected incident. The reason is that a person who has trained oneself to be economical in normal circumstances is more capable of managing a crisis. To the contrary, a person who is not economical in normal circumstances will collapse when a tragedy strikes.

It has been narrated that Imam Ali (a) said:

> The power of reason dictates that you should become economical not wasteful, that you do not break your promise, and that you suppress your anger.[294]

A sound and reasonable person is indeed one who is economical

[292] Ibid., vol. 2, p. 136, ch. 73,trad. 61.

[293] Ibid., vol. 2, p. 233, ch. 77, trad. 1391.

[294] Ibid., vol. 1, p. 116, ch. 1, trad. 2152.

instead of being wasteful, and one who makes promises but does not break them, and is one who suppresses one's anger. A person who is not economical is accordingly not sound; and the same applies to one who breaks promises and does not suppress his anger. Furthermore, just as the intellect calls on being economical, magnanimity also calls on being economical.

Imam Ali (a) says:

> Magnanimity entails that a person becomes economical, not wasteful; and that one makes promises but does not break them.[295]

Magnanimity (*muruwwah* in Arabic) means - as explained in the book *Duroos* - that a person "exalts oneself from the types of ignobility which are not suitable for someone in one stature, such as joking or eating in the market, or for a religious scholar to wear an army outfit if that invites ridicule or mockery."[296]

Therefore, being wasteful is a type of ignobility and lowliness, unlike being economical which indicates a noble and lofty spirit. Imam Ali (a) says:

> A person who is not adept at being economical will perish by being wasteful.[297]

Being economical is the key to wellness and success, unlike being wasteful, as the one who is not adept at being economical will perish by being wasteful. It is possible that being "economical" as mentioned in the hadith is not confined to money or time—by not wasting it—but also includes being economical in using one's physical capabilities and also using appliances and various types of equipment.

Imam Ali (a) says:

> Being economical generates wealth, while being wasteful/

---

[295] Ibid., vol. 2, p. 256, ch. 78, trad. 140.

[296] Al-Shaheed al-Awwal quotes this definition in his book *Duroos* from the book *Majma' al-Bahrain* under the root word "*mara.*"

[297] *Ghurar al-Hikam*, vol. 2, p. 178, ch. 77, trad. 561.

> extravagant causes deprivation.[298]

It is possible that the reason why being economical generates wealth—and also accordingly protects wealth from being wasted or squandered—is because being economical is a general inclination or condition, just like other psychological conditions.

Therefore, if one learns to be economical in one aspect of life, then one will generally be economical in other aspects as well. Such a person will enjoy a balanced life which is based on wisdom, and will achieve success and consequently become wealthy from different dimensions as well, and vice-versa.

You Must Manage Your Life Properly

Imam Ali (a) says:

> If Allah wants goodness for one of His servants, then He will inspire that person to be economical and to efficiently manage his life, and He will protect him from mismanagement and being wasteful.[299]

Being "inspired" by Allah is undoubtedly a Divine grace, but Allah has also assigned certain means to achieve results. From this, we come to understand why Allah wills goodness for certain people and not others, for if a servant of Allah makes the effort, asks, learns, supplicates to Allah and implores Him, then Allah will inspire that person to become economical and to manage one's affairs efficiently, and He will protect them from mismanagement and being wasteful.

Therefore, the "inspiration" that this person receives from Allah is the reward one earned for the efforts that were exerted, such as making the effort to learn, plan and supplicate. Allah says in the Holy Quran:

> Then he followed another cause.[300]

---

[298] *Al-Kafi*, vol. 4, p. 52, trad. 4.

[299] *Ghurar al-Hikam*, vol. 1, p. 285, ch. 16, trad. 164.

[300] *Quran*, Surah al-Kahf (18), verse 89.

He also says:

> If you support Allah, then He will support you.[301]

In another verse, He says:

> And Allah increases in guidance those who seek guidance.[302]

To the contrary, Allah says:

> They have forgotten Allah, so He has forgotten them.[303]

For this reason, the Commander of the Faithful Imam Ali (a) said:

> Adorn yourselves with chastity/purity, and avoid squandering and being wasteful.[304]

Become a Businessman and Avoid Being Employed

Imam al-Sadiq (a) said: The non-Arabs went to the Commander of the Faithful Imam Ali (a) and said:

> We have a complain to you from the Arabs! The Messenger of Allah (s) used to give us the same that he would give them, and he married off Salman, Bilal, and Suhaib (to Arab women) but now they have refused to give us their daughters. Imam Ali (a) went to them (the Arabs) and discussed with them this matter. The Arabs shouted: We refuse O Abal Hasan, we refuse. The Imam (a) left in a state of anger while saying: O non-Arabs, these people (the Arabs) have treated you like the Jews and Christians. They marry your daughters but they refuse to give you their daughters, and they do not give you what they take from you. Therefore, go and become businessmen, for I heard the Messenger of Allah (s) say, 'Sustenance has ten

---

[301] *Quran*, Surah Muhammad (47), verse 7.

[302] *Quran*, Surah Maryam (19), verse 76.

[303] *Quran*, Surah al-Tawbah (9), verse 67.

[304] Ibid., vol. 1, p. 347, ch. 28, trad. 82.

> parts; nine parts lie in doing business and one part is in other things.'[305]

This *hadith* makes a number of important points, such as the following:

1. The Imam (a) would take it upon himself to solve the problems of the people, he was very down to earth, and he would live among the people (unlike kings who are isolated from the general public).
2. The humbleness of the Imam, who is God's proof over all creations, as he himself went to address the Arabs.
3. The Imam took it upon himself to offer economic advice to the non-Arabs.
4. It is incumbent on the lower and middle classes to start up businesses or trade so that they can protect themselves from being marginalized, sidelined, socially isolated and exploited.

It is also incumbent on Muslim leaders, scholars, speakers, intellectuals and professors to follow the example of Imam Ali (a) in all of these regards.

Imam Ali (a) says:

> Bring yourself to do business, for it provides you richness from needing what people have.[306]

It appears from this and other *ahadith* that if a person had to choose between being employed or starting his own business, then one should start his own business because the one who is employed is held captive to his job and is at the mercy of his boss or the company that he works for. He is always at risk of losing his job and so he has no employment security.

As for doing business, it means that one can serve and contribute more and more, and it also means that one becomes

[305] *Al-Kafi*, vol. 5, p. 318, trad. 59.

[306] *Wasa'il al-Shia*, vol. 12, p. 5, ch. 1, trad. 11.

self-sufficient and no longer needs assistance from others.[307]

Travel or Migrate

Imam Ali (a) says that the Messenger of Allah (s) said:

> If you run into financial difficulties (become poor), set out from your home, travel, seek the blessings of Allah, and do not cause grief to yourself and your family.[308]

Traveling and migrating are two wide gates for seeking sustenance, so it is incumbent on the poor and those with limited income to travel to other cities or countries, or migrate to them if they do not have any opportunities in their own cities. If they do that, then the doors which they had not anticipated will open up for them. Here are some possible reasons for that:

1. There could be new opportunities in new environments.
2. Traveling and migrating free an individual from many social restrictions that bog him down, and so without such restrictions (in a new environment), one is able to take off and excel.
3. Traveling and migrating reveal to a person one's abilities and

[307] It is evident that we do not suggest all people should leave their jobs and go into business, and that is why we said "if one were to choose between being employed or starting his own business." What we mean is that if one is employed simply so his job serves as his source of income, then it is better for him to go into business provided that the conditions for being successful in business are there. As for those who fill specific roles and have special expertise in the fields of physics, chemistry, medicine, engineering, advanced technology, and scientific and academic research, what we said does not apply to them, as it is obligatory for a group of people to fill these important roles - just like doing business, and they may even be more important than doing business. What is required is for the business sector and these specialized fields to complete and complement each other so that a flourishing nation and a happy society are built.

[308] *Da'a'em al-Islam*, vol. 2, p. 13, ch. 1, trad. 1.

strengths, or remind a person about one's capabilities and strengths, or give one the opportunity to use them and take off.

4. Migration represents a big challenge, and in big challenges a human develops oneself and their capabilities, strengthens one's will, and exploits one's apparent and inherent powers - all of which represent the key to advancement.

Perfect Your Work and be Cautious

Imam Ali (a) said in describing the livelihood of people:

> As for (the importance of) doing business, Allah says: 'O you who believe, whenever you contract a debt from one another for a known term, commit it to writing...'[309]

Allah, the Almighty instructed them how to buy goods whether traveling or in their homeland; and how to do business, since it is one of the ways to make a living."[310]

Perfecting one's work and being cautious are among the most important qualities a businessman, merchant or one who is on he path to becoming a businessman should have. One way to perfect one's work is to write or record a debt and other transactions. They must be recorded in secure registries. Being careless to document such transactions, on the other hand, can lead to the destruction of companies, and lead to bankruptcy as well.

Invest Even in a Seed

It has been narrated that Imam al-Sadiq (a) said:

> The Commander of the Faithful (a) used to cultivate the land with a shovel, and the Messenger of Allah (s) used to suck the seed in his mouth and plant it, and it would immediately germinate. The Commander of the Faithful

---

[309] *Quran*, Surah al-Baqarah (2) verse 282.

[310] *Wasa'il al-Shia*, vol. 12, p. 4, ch. 1, trad. 7.

> freed 1,000 slaves from his money and hard work.[311]

We conclude the following from this *hadith*:

1. Work is honorable and dignified, whatever it may be. Those from the upper classes and from the noble families should not see that their status makes it inappropriate for them to work, even if they work with a shovel.
2. It is necessary to invest in or utilize even a seed and not be wasteful even to this small extent, by not throwing a seed away and sucking it before planting it.
3. It is necessary to use money for a good purpose and spend it on that which benefits people and society. It is also necessary to exert ample effort to liberate the lower and exploited class, and among the most important examples is emancipating slaves.

Invest in Agriculture

It has been reported that Imam Ali (a):

> ...used to work with his hands, fight in the way of Allah until he would secure what Allah had bestowed on him, and he would be seen with a caravan of camels loaded with seeds. He would be asked, 'What is this, O Abal Hasan?' He would reply, 'Palm trees by the will of Allah.' Then he would plant them all leaving not a single seed. He was steadfast about fighting in the way of Allah during the days of the Messenger of Allah (s); when he rose (to the caliphate) by the request of the people; and until Allah took his soul. In between those times he would work his fields (or farmlands) with his hands until he set free 1,000 slaves, all of them from the money that he earned with his own two hands.[312]

[311] *Al-Kafi*, vol. 5, p. 74, trad. 2.

[312] *Da'a'em al-Islam*, vol. 2, p. 302, ch. 1, trad. 1133.

We conclude from this narration and others the following:

1. It is recommended to work with one's hands, as the Imam (a) worked with his hands.
2. It is recommended to farm or cultivate land even for scholars and businessmen, as working with one's hands and farming leads to a healthy and physically fit body and mind. In addition, it makes a human being humble and introduces one to the life of the underprivileged and the difficulties that they experience, making one sympathetic to them. It also makes a person aware of the blessings that Allah has bestowed upon him through the money which he has earned from easier or more convenient methods. Consequently, one will be less likely to squander one's own money or spend it on prohibited causes.
3. It is necessary to be diligent and hardworking. Imam Ali (a) "was seen with a caravan of camels loaded with seeds." How difficult it must have been to plant all of those seeds!
4. It is necessary not to waste anything, even if it is something which appears insignificant like a seed.
5. It is necessary to continue working and to not quit, without making up any excuses to rest or retire, and thus we see that Imam Ali (a) would "work his fields (or farmlands) in between those times."
6. It is necessary to share your wealth with others and make them happy, and therefore the Imam (a) "emancipated 1,000 slaves, all of them with the money that he made from working with his own hands."
7. It is incumbent on the Imam and the believers to struggle in the way of Allah and in the way of those who are poor or exploited whenever it is necessary.

You Should be Self-Sufficient in Your Home

It has been narrated that Imam al-Sadiq (a) said:

> The Commander of the Faithful (a) would gather firewood, bring water from the well, and broom the house; and Lady Fatima (a) would grind (barley), knead, and bake the bread.[313]

Among the factors that decrease costs is for a husband to help his wife with the house chores, divide the duties in the house, and keep away from employing domestic servants as much as possible. All of this makes it more possible to meet a family's needs at home with the least cost, and this serves to reduce pressure on the poor and allows them to take a step towards achieving a surplus which will come to their aid in times of tragedy or hardship. It also allows them to end up with some capital which will help them in investing.

The narration mentioned above is confirmed by other narrations such as a narration by Imam al-Baqir (a) in which he says:

> (Lady) Fatima (a) made an agreement with (Imam) Ali (a) to take care of the house chores, knead, bake the bread, and broom the house,[314] and (Imam) Ali (a) agreed to take care of what is beyond the door such as gathering firewood, bringing food, and so on...[315]

---

[313] *Wasa'il al-Shia*, vol. 12, p. 24, ch. 9, trad. 10.

[314] One way to reconcile this narration with the previous one which stated that the Imam would broom the house is that this one is talking about a certain period and that one is about another period, based on different circumstances such as their health. Another way to reconcile them is to say that she had promised him to take care of brushing the house, but this does not mean that sometimes or often even he would not do that to help her out.

[315] *Tafsir al-Ayyashi*, vol. 1, p. 171, trad. 41, in the exegesis of Surah Ale Imran.

This narration does not mean that a woman is only reduced to house chores such as cooking. What is meant is that a woman must not be arrogant to do such chores, and neither should the man (as it will be demonstrated in the next heading under "Help your Spouses"), as it is demonstrated by Imam Ali's (a) approach in the division of labor between himself and his respected wife Lady Fatima (a). The wellbeing, goodness, blessings and solidarity of a family all depend on both spouses working and helping out at home.

It is important to note that a wife is not obligated to do the house chores, and according to Islamic Law, she has the right to ask her husband to pay her for cooking, cleaning, taking care of the kids, and such activities, just like any other work she does whether at home or outside of the house. However, doing all of this without asking to be paid is a definite factor in keeping the family coherent and solidifying the bonds of love and compassion. It will also help reduce financial costs.

A man must appreciate the value and sanctity of a woman and her willingness to do the house chores for free, since she is not obligated to do them, and thus he should treat her with even more love, respect and appreciation. Consequently, the atmosphere at home will turn into one of faith, love, tranquility, compassion and morality.

A man must also not prevent his wife from working at home or outside—alongside managing the house—if her work is appropriate and protects her chastity, honor, dignity and purity; and it does not conflict with her marital obligations or raising their own children.

Some examples of such work are teaching, being a nurse—within the Islamic framework—writing scholarly papers, seeking education, being a member of strategic studies centers, directing schools, colleges, and academies dedicated for women or girls only, or other things provided that she observes the Islamic conditions such as "be not soft in your speech lest he in whose heart is a disease be moved with desire."[316]

Other examples (of appropriate work) include sewing, knitting, embroidery, drawing, engraving, programming, dubbing, and other types of work related to computers, producing documentaries, and so on. Some other examples include helping her husband or sons on the farm or in their company.

However, it is upon the government and society to provide work opportunities for women that minimize mixing with men in corporations, schools, hospitals, and other institutions. This will grant women greater freedom and convenience to move, such as in female schools or hospitals, and it will also better protect their chastity and honor. It will also offer greater assurance that those with weak self-restraint will not cross the lines of chastity and honor, since though it is not prohibited for a woman to work in an environment in which men exist as long as the chastity, purity, and *hijab* are observed. This point requires a separate discussion, and if Allah Wills, then we will address this in another book in detail.

It is important to note that Lady Fatima's (a) work at home, in addition to it being recommended, served to demonstrate that she did not distinguish herself over other women of the world. Most of the people in Medina were poor, and so Lady Fatima (a) set the best example for the daughters and wives of leaders, emirs, rulers, ministers and public officials to live just like most people live, and to endure hardships just like most women do in their city - whether it is enduring the heat or cold, difficulties, hard work, fatigue or enduring various activities. She set the example for them so they would not act arrogantly and superior to other people, live an extravagant life, be wasteful, travel and have fun, while less fortunate people taste the pain of hunger and lack the basic needs of life.

It is also important to note that Lady Fatima (a) assumed the role of a religious and social teacher and educator, and we have

---

316 *Quran*, Surah al-Ahzab (33) verse 32.

many narrations about this. She also assumed a major strategic political role, among them being her standing up to the big coup that ensued after the martyrdom of her chosen father, Prophet Muhammad (s).[317]

Help your Spouse

Helping one's spouse earns the satisfaction of the Lord, earns a great reward, and leads to greater productivity. How wonderful is this hadith by Imam Ali (a) in which he says:

> Once the Messenger of Allah (s) entered upon us while Fatima (a) was sitting by the pot and I was peeling lentils from their skin. The Messenger said: 'O Abal Hasan.' I replied: 'Here I am at your service.' He then said: 'Listen, and whatever I say is an instruction by my Lord. Any man who helps his wife at home, for every hair on his body, he will receive the reward of fasting an entire year during the day and praying an entire year at night...O Ali, helping one's spouse is an expiation for grave sins, extinguishes the anger of the Lord, is the dowry for *Hoor al-Ayn,* increases one's good deeds, and elevates one's status. O Ali, only the one who is steadfast in truthfulness, a martyr, or one for whom Allah wants the goodness of the world and the Hereafter will help his family.'[318]

There are many benefits for men helping their spouses, whether those men are businessmen, scholars, students, professors, doctors, lawyers, engineers, rulers or subjects. Some of the benefits include strengthening the bonds of love in the family which yields cohesion and solidarity in the family. Consequently, love, compassion, tranquility and peace will envelop the family, and the rates of divorce will decrease to the lowest. Children will

[317] Refer to the book *Min Fiqh al-Zahra,* the book *Fatima Bahjato Qalb al-Mustafa* and the book *Fatimat al-Zahra min al-Mahde ila al-Lahdi.*

[318] *Mustadrak al-Wasa'il,* vol. 13, p. 48, ch. 17, trad. 2, which cites *Jame' al-Akhbaar,* p. 102.

have the best upbringing, crimes such as theft and harassment will drop, and suicide rates will also drop.

These crimes or vices are generally the products of broken families and disputes between the parents, both of which produce children full of anger, hatred, aggression and other moral vices. Furthermore, among the most important positive effects to everyone is that the family will be blessed with economic security and financial stability. For this reason and other reasons, this great reward has been assigned to those who help their spouses at home or outside of the home.

Work and Work

It has been narrated that Imam al-Sadiq (a) said:

> The Messenger of Allah (s) said: When Allah (s) had Adam (a) descend from heaven (down to earth), He instructed him to cultivate (the ground) with his hands and eat from the work of his hands, after having had the blessings of heaven...[319]

This is an announcement and declaration from the Almighty Allah that the world is based on work and labor, and this is how a human being prepares his way to heaven anew. Therefore, you must work and work hard!

Invest in Water and Land

It has been narrated that Imam al-Sadiq (a) quoted his father Imam al-Baqir (a) saying:

> The Commander of the Faithful (a) used to say: "A person one who finds water and earth but then finds himself in need, Allah will keep away from him (and thus he should not blame but himself)."[320]

Water and earth are raw resources or materials for wealth and

[319] *Mustadrak al-Wasa'il*, vol. 13, p. 24, ch. 8, trad. 9.

[320] *Qurb al-Isnaad*, p. 115, trad. 404.

richness, and it is "work" that transforms them into wealth. Therefore, if Allah grants you these raw materials and you do not work and became poor, then Allah will keep you away from His mercy, benefaction, and favors due to your negligence and poor choice.

Just as this applies to individuals, it also applies to nations, for a nation that owns water and land but then falls in need to other countries for agricultural products and imports even wheat and barley, is a nation that has been kept away from the mercy of Allah due to its negligence and poor choice.

Adopt the System of Delegating and Division of Labor

Imam al-Sadiq (a) says:

> Execute your major tasks yourself, but delegate your minor tasks to others.[321]

Among the most important ways to achieve success, progress and become wealthy is the policy of delegating and division of labor. Thus, Imam al-Sadiq (a) states:

> Delegate your minor tasks to others.

What is strange is that we see some people marginalize others even when it comes to minor and secondary issues, and they personally want to manage and administer everything directly and execute all responsibilities! We deduce from this *hadith* that among the most important methods to advance trade and investment is for a person to observe a combination of the following:

1. Delegate the tasks to others that do not have to be executed by one personally.
2. Personally execute important tasks instead of avoiding them or neglecting them.

---

[321] *Awali al-Li'ali*, vol. 3, p. 197, trad. 13.

Learn the Laws of Trading

Learning the laws of trading and doing business serves as a guarantee to achieving honesty, integrity, uprightness and richness.

Once a man said to Imam Ali (a):

> O Commander of the Faithful, I want to trade. The Imam said to him: Have you learned the laws of Allah's religion? The man replied: Some of them. The Imam then told him: Woe unto you! You must learn then you can trade, for the one who buys and sells without knowing what is lawful and what is unlawful will collide with usury and collide.[322]

Learning and practicing Islamic laws secures uprightness, honesty, integrity, justice; and an increase, development and blessing of resources. A person who does not learn the laws of religion, or does not know what is lawful and what is unlawful will fall into the pits of financial corruption, such as cheating, deception, bribery, fraud, hoarding, illegitimate monopolization, oppression, unfairness and usury. The Imam (a) mentioned usury only as an example. in the above narration.

It is evident that learning the laws of religion is only one condition to avoid committing that which is unlawful; and the second part is to have faith so that a businessman and trader can keep a distance from that which is unlawful.

Furthermore, learning the laws of trading and doing business does not mean that every businessman, trader or skilled worker should become a jurist. What is meant, however, is that they must have awareness about their dealings and the religious laws which concern their transactions, and if they are not aware of all of the rulings that concern them, then they should consult jurists, their representatives or their books. With financial justice, honesty, integrity and uprightness, wealth and resources

---

[322] *Da'a'em al-Islam*, vol. 2, p. 16, ch. 1, trad. 12.

will multiply and develop, and Allah will bless them with lasting goodness.

Appoint the Qualified

The Commander of the Faithful Imam Ali (a) used to say:

> Only those who understand well buying and selling should sit in the market.[323]

It appears that the Imam's instruction is an advisory instruction, not a religious instruction[324] even though it is possible that it is a religious commandment. However, even if it is a religious instruction, then it is not unlawful for others to sit in the market unless if it leads them to commit that which is unlawful.

It is understood from the hadith that it is not desired (*makrooh*) to delegate the task of buying or selling to someone who does not properly understand buying and selling. Therefore, those who are not familiar with the system of buying and selling and how it works should not sit in the market and do business, buy or sell.

Hold on to Supplication then Inspiration

It has been narrated that Imam Ali (a) said in the *Hadith of the 400*,[325] that:

> If you want to buy something from the market, then as you enter the market say, 'I bear witness that there is no god but Allah, the One who has no partner; and I bear witness that Muhammad (s) is His slave and messenger.

[323] *Al-Kafi*, vol. 5, p. 154, trad. 23.

[324] The difference is that a religious instruction is either compulsory or recommended. If it is compulsory, then violating it constitutes a sin, and if it is recommended, then not following it is religiously not obligatory. An advisory instruction, however, is simply advice, and it does not carry religious weight to it.

[325] This is a well-known hadith attributed to Imam Ali (a) in which he gives 400 valuable recommendations, many of which address healthy living and eating.

> O Allah, I seek refuge in You from a loss-making deal, and from a false oath; and I seek refuge in You from absolute loss or failure.'[326]

When a businessman or merchant prays and says:

> O Allah, I seek refuge in you from a loss-making deal, a false oath...

he is achieving the following objectives:

First: He is seeking the rain of Allah's mercy, the One in whose hands is giving sustenance, just as all of the creation are in His hands.

Second: He is going through the process of seeking inspiration by being mindful to avoid damaging transactions and trying to make profit through sinful ways and false oaths. Such supplications educate a human being to adopt the culture of making a lawful profit, and to avoid unlawful means of making a living and disastrous deals.

Remember the Almighty Allah

It has been narrated that Imam Ali (a) said in the *Hadith of the 400*:

> Constantly remember Allah when you enter the market and people are busy, for doing so expiates your sins, increases your good deeds, and you will not be recorded among those who are oblivious.[327]

Maintaining a balance between this world and the hereafter is among the most important factors in achieving progress and happiness, which positively reflects on the economic productivity of individuals. Constantly mentioning and remembering Allah the Almighty minimizes the chances of committing that which is economically unlawful and which harms the businessman himself just as it harms those who are deprived. Some examples

---

[326] *Al-Khisaal*, vol. 2, p. 634, trad. 10, the *Hadith of the 400.*

[327] Ibid., vol. 2, p. 614, trad. 10, the *Hadith of the 400.*

of harmful transactions include usury or interest, hoarding or unlawful monopolization, unfairness, bribery, fraud and so on.

Be Lenient, for it is the Path to Profitability

Imam Ali (a) said:

> I heard the Messenger of Allah saying: 'Being Lenient is a type of profitability.'[328]

Being lenient means ease in conducting a transaction. Being lenient, easy, not complicating matters, and not being too tough are all among the most important factors which attracts clients.

Give More and You Will Make More

It has been narrated that Imam al-Sadiq (a) said:

> Once the Commander of the Faithful (a) passed by a female servant who bought meat from a butcher while saying 'give me more.' The Commander of the Faithful told the butcher, 'Give her more, for it is the greatest blessing.'[329]

Doing good to others is among the methods of creating social solidarity and stability, which positively reflects on the general economic output. Giving the buyer more brings about blessings as the hadith states.

The word "*barakah*" used in the *hadith*, which means blessing, denotes an increase in quantity, an improvement in quality, and deep-rootedness, and it also denotes purity. Blessings have two dimensions:

Divine Dimension: Giving the buyer will more bring about the mercy and compassion of Allah, and Allah will give more good to those who are good.

Natural or Material Dimension: Giving the buyer more is an ideal way to attract more and more clients, which in turn will

[328] *Man La Yahdharoh al-Faqih*, vol. 3, p. 122, ch. 61, trad. 19.

[329] *Al-Kafi*, vol. 5, p. 152, trad. 8.

increase profits. Even though the profit margin decreases (by giving more to the buyer), the overall revenue will be greater (leading to greater overall profit).

Choose a Unique Location

Imam Ali (a) says:

> The Prophet (s) once passed by a man who wanted to sell some goods. The Prophet (s) said to him: 'Go to the beginning of the market.'[330]

Businessmen, traders, skilled workers and craftsmen should all learn the art and way of marketing, and one example of this is to choose a strategic location as the tradition points out. This tradition also clearly demonstrates to us that the Prophet (s) did not limit his interactions with people to religious guidance only, he also exercised his role as an economic mentor, teacher and advisor, just as Allah stateed in the Holy Quran that the Prophet:

> ...is tender and merciful to the believers.[331]

Avoid Taking an Oath in the Name of Allah

It has been narrated that Imam Ali (a) would say:

> Beware of taking oaths, for it causes your goods to wear out and keeps blessings away from you.[332]

The one who takes an oath in order to market his product is either truthful or lying. If he is lying, then in addition to bringing about the wrath of Allah upon himself, he will lose credibility throughout time, and therefore less people will want to deal with him. If he is truthful in his oath, then his "goods will wear out" due to the oath.

The reason could be that in addition to the inappropriateness

---

[330] *Man La Yahdharoh al-Faqih*, vol. 3, p. 122, ch. 61, trad. 23.

[331] *Quran*, Surah al-Tawbah (9), verse 128

[332] *Al-Kafi*, vol. 5, p. 162, trad. 4.

of swearing by Allah, as it is demeaning to the majestic name of Allah (for He is much greater than the matters on which we take an oath in His name) that the one who tries to market his goods by swearing in God's name may not be too concerned about the quality of his goods because he will try to compensate for that by taking an oath in Allah. This will cause him to keep regressing in regards to the quality of his goods.

Take Care of Your Possessions

It has been narrated that Abu Matar said:

> I left the *masjid* and suddenly a man behind me called out saying, 'Raise your garment, for it is more lasting for your garment and it is more pious for you to do so.' I followed him, and he was wearing a garment and a cloak and was carrying a stick, resembling an Arab Bedouin. I asked, 'Who is this?' A man replied to me saying, 'It seems you are a stranger in this city.' I said, 'Yes, I am from the city of Basra.' Then the man told me, 'This person (the one who called him) is Ali the Commander of the Faithful (a).'[333]

Among the most important ways to cut back on spending is to take proper care of one's possessions so that they last longer and remain in good condition. Raising one's garment, as mentioned in the tradition, is a good example of that, for it is more lasting for a garment as it protects it from brushing the ground, stones and thorns, which eventually could tear the garment or at least make it dirty. As for the Imam (a) saying that doing so is "more pious for you," it is because raising one's garment protects it from being contaminated by filth and religious impurities (*najasaat*).

Avoid False Marketing

It has been narrated that Imam al-Sadiq (a) quoted his father (a) saying:

[333] *Bihar al-Anwar*, vol. 40, p. 331, ch. 98, trad. 14.

> The Messenger of Allah (s) said, 'Allah will not address three people, He will not pronounce them pure, and they will have a painful punishment: The one who acts arrogantly; the one who falsely advertises his goods; and the one who greets you (warmly) with an open chest but he conceals his true feelings and his heart is full of deception.'[334]

False advertising might encourage people to buy from you more and more, but in the long run, or even in the meantime, false advertising is considered among the primary causes of economic failure.

Avoid Fraud or Deception

In the book *al-Ja'fariyyat*, it is narrated that Imam Ali (a) mounted the Prophet's (s) mule called "*Shahbaa*'" in the city of Kufa, and then he passed by each market until he came across the date sellers and told them:

> Display your poor or low-grade goods just as you display the good quality ones. Then he came across the fish sellers and told them: Only sell that which is good and fresh, and beware of selling fish that were found [dead] floating in the water.

Honesty is considered among the most important factors that ensure a healthy economy, and among the most important examples is avoiding fraud or deception. Deception is a vice whether it is small or big.

Work in Your Hometown

In the book *al-Ja'fariyyat*, it is narrated that Imam Ali (a) said:

> The Messenger of Allah said: 'Among the blessings of a person which make one blissful are righteous friends, an obedient and good child, a compliant wife, and to make a

[334] *Makarim al-Akhlaaq*, p. 111.

> living in one's hometown.'[335]

Healthy planning is the key to a blessed sustenance and a pleasant life, and an example of good planning is to make a living in your hometown, for that brings bliss and happiness. Working in an unfamiliar environment or in places where one is a stranger comes with difficulties which might cause depression, stress and various types of diseases. It can also lead the migrant himself or some members of his family to become corrupt; or it could lead to the breakup of the family, or the inability of the head of the household to properly raise the family and give them the required emotional support.

This is the basis and general rule, but if one runs into a dead end and cannot find means to make a living, then he may have to move or migrate, but he must plan well so that he is protected from the complications of migration or frequent traveling as much as he can. Allah has promised to compensate the one who migrates for His cause with great and ample blessings. As the Quran says:

> And whoever migrates in Allah's way will find in the earth many a place of refuge and abundant resources, and whoever goes forth from one's house migrating to Allah and His Messenger, and then death overtakes him, his reward is indeed with Allah and Allah is Forgiving, Merciful.[336]

Make a Partnership with the Successful and the Fortunate

Imam Ali (a) said:

> Become a partner with the one who has abundant sustenance, for it is more likely to bring about richness

[335] *Mustadrak al-Wasa'il*, vol. 13, p. 292, ch. 41, trad. 1, narrating from *al-Ja'fariyyat*, p. 194.

[336] *Quran*, Surah al-Nisa (4), verse 100.

> and make one fortunate.[337]

Based on this *hadith*, a merchant or businessman must:

1. Thoroughly study the market and monitor the commercial or economic moves that businessmen and companies make so that he can determine who the successful ones are, the secret behind their success, and the factors which led them to their fortune.
2. Try to become close to them and befriend them.
3. Make a partnership contract with them or make some sort of broad alliance with them, so that you can take off to more expansive economic horizons, by the will of Allah.

Wisely Choose who You Ask for Help

Imam Ali (a) says:

> O my dear son, if the paucity of time and scarcity of life befall you, then seek help from those who have firm roots and a fixed origin, from the people of mercy, empathy, and compassion, for they can better fulfill your needs and solve your problems.[338]

If you become unemployed, lose your work or need intensive consultation during a financial crisis that you are going through, or if you need a loan or a legitimate mediation to remove obstacles in the way of your business, then as the Imam (a) instructs, 'wisely choose those who you want help from in solving your problems and fulfilling your need.' Otherwise, those who you ask help from will exacerbate your situation and make you more miserable.

The Imam (a) also guides us to the standard or criteria that you should observe when considering from whom to seek help. We must ponder well on the five qualities that the Imam (a)

---

[337] *Nahj al-Balagha*, maxim 230.

[338] *A'laam al-Deen*, p. 274.

mentioned.

Do not Deal with the Indecent

Imam Ali (a) says in the *Hadith of the 400* that:

> Beware those who are indecent, for the indecent ones are those who do not fear Allah (a). Among them are the killers of prophets, and among them are our enemies.[339]

Cheating, betrayal, theft and deception are among the most important factors which lead people and companies to making losses, and they usually lead to bankruptcy as well. Therefore, it is incumbent on traders and businessmen to avoid dealing with indecent people and employing them, because they are the people who betray, cheat, deceive and embezzle the most.

How many a time have people lost everything that they have, failed in their businesses, made big losses, or closed down their factories and shops because of the betrayal or disloyalty of an indecent employee, co-worker, or partner!

Who are the indecent people? In this hadith, Imam Ali (a) explains who they are:

> If you do not care about what you say or what is said about you, then you are indecent.[340]

The "indecent" ones are those who have no dignity or honor, and therefore they are not concerned about what they say about people, such as the slanders, accusations, backbiting, insults and attacks that they make against people. They are also not concerned about the criticisms, attacks and the (negative) disclosures that people make about them. This is a dangerous sign that indicates such people are not deterred from betraying or committing crimes such as theft, embezzlement, manipulation of the market, and so on.

---

[339] *Al-Khisaal*, vol. 2, p. 635, trad. 10, *Hadith of the 400.*

[340] Refer to *Tahdhib al-Ahkam*, vol. 6, p. 295, ch. 92, trad. 28.

Go to Work Early

Imam Ali (a) says:

> When you finish the morning prayer, then go seek sustenance early in the morning.[341]

Being active is the key to success, and among the components of success is to seek sustenance early in the morning, and the best time is right after finishing the morning prayer. Therefore be active, go out to work early, and God Willing, you will achieve your goals.

Uphold Reliability and Perfection

Imam Ali (a) stood by a tailor and said:

> O tailor, may bereaved mothers grieve over you! Make the threads solid, make your stitches exact, and make the piercings close to one another, for I heard the Messenger of Allah (s) say: 'Allah will resurrect the deceptive tailor wearing a shirt and robe which he sewed with deception; and beware of leftover or unused pieces (of thread or cloth), for the owner of the garment is more rightful to them, and do not consider them as compensation for your work.'[342]

Trustworthiness and perfection are two conditions among the conditions of success, and they also serve as the basis for receiving Divine reward; contrary to deception and negligence,[343] for they serve as the basis of Divine punishment.

A tailor is only an example mentioned in the tradition, but the same applies to other skilled workers and professionals, such as blacksmiths, butchers, goldsmiths, jewelers, engineers, doctors,

---

[341] *Al-Kafi*, vol. 5, p. 79, trad. 8.

[342] *Tanbih al-Khawatir*, p. 42.

[343] Negligence or carelessness which leads to the violation of the rights of others.

and lawyers. They must all perfect their work and be concise to the greatest extent possible, and they must all be trustworthy as best as one can be.

Continue Work and Production even if You are not in Need

According to a tradition Imam Ali (a) used to go out during midday heat even though he was not in need, but he wanted Allah to see him tiring himself seeking lawful sustenance.[344]

A society that works hard and produces well is a society which Allah loves. Thus, Imam Ali (a) used to go out during midday heat to work even though he was not in need of it. What would the Imam (a) do with the extra money he would make? He would spend it on the poor, the destitute, orphans and widows - and this is how we must always be!

Settle for What is Necessary

Imam Ali (a) said:

> The bare minimum (which helps you to live) is sufficient.[345]

Cutting back on spending is recommended, but if not cutting back on spending leads to being wasteful or squandering, then it becomes prohibited to not cut back on spending. This tradition which says that the bare minimum is sufficient means that one should be content with fulfilling one's basic needs, and cutting back on spending means to be content with what is necessary.

A person's way of life should not be to pursue gaining more and more simply because one wants to go with the flow.

One of the common mistakes that we see among many of the youth is their obsession with the latest gadgets[346] and devices

---

[344] *Man La Yahdharah al-Faqih*, vol. 3, p. 99, ch. 58, trad. 31.

[345] *Nahj al-Balagha*, maxim 395.

[346] Such as their obsession with the latest model of the iPhone, iPod, or Galaxy line of Smartphones, their computers or other devices, and also the obsession of many women with womens' accessories and home

even though they do not need them. They simply want to go with the new trend and boast in front of their friends!

Be Easygoing and do not be Stern

Imam Ali (a) says:

> Be compliant with the world as long as it is in your grip.[347]

One of the ways to success is to avoid being stern. Instead, be easygoing or mellow when dealing with others. According to one tradition, the Children of Israel complicated their own matters, so Allah complicated matters for them even more, but had they made things easy, then Allah would have made things easy for them too.[348]

Being easygoing or lenient means that one is flexible when buying, selling, renting, leasing, and cancelling a transaction, without the complications of administrative or bureaucratic routine. Therefore, if things come to you easily, then be easy with people so that this blessing lasts for you.

Beware of Laziness

Imam Ali (a) said:

> One whose laziness is persistent will not realize his hopes and his deeds will be unfavorable.[349]

The one who is lazy will have bad deeds (accumulate) and at the same time he will not fulfill his goals. The one who is lazy will disregard working, or if he works, his work will be poor and sloppy. Therefore, he will not realize his hopes and goals as a

---

furnishings or appliances.

[347] *Nahj al-Balagha*, letter 31 which he wrote to his son Imam al-Hasan (a) after the battle of Siffeen.

[348] Refer to *Uyun al-Akhbar al-Ridha (a)*, vol. 1, p. 16, trad. 31. It is a long narration addressing the incident of the cow and the Children of Israel. There is a phrase in it which says: "They complicated things, so Allah complicated things on them."

[349] *Ghurar al-Hikam*, vol. 2, p. 162, ch. 77, trad. 263.

natural consequence to that.

Imam Ali (a) says:

> When things became coupled, laziness was coupled with inability, and from them poverty was born.[350]

This is a practical, applied equation: laziness + inability = poverty. As for the one who is incapable, with effort he can create power, ability and strength. Consequently, he will not remain incapable. As for the one who is capable but lazy, he is like a lazy inheritor who inherits a large fortune, but then quickly squanders or wastes his fortune.

Avoid Baseless Wishes and Turn to Work

Imam Ali (a) said in his will to his son Muhammad ibn al-Hanafiyya:

> My son, never rely on baseless wishes for they are the goods of the foolish and inhibit or dispirit you from the Hereafter...The noblest richness is avoiding baseless wishes.[351]

One of the factors which lead to poverty is relying or banking on baseless wishes and hopes. Instead of planning, working, striving and being diligent, some people live in a world of dreams and wishes. This is a recipe for failure and is a weapon of the foolish in facing the world and its difficulties.

Pursue Positive Dreams

In the book *al-Ja'fariyyat*, it is narrated that Imam Ali (a) said:

> If one of you wants to wish for something, then wish for a lot of goodness, for Allah is generous and munificent.[352]

Wishing for success and advancement is good and desired

---

[350] *Al-Kafi*, vol. 5, p. 86, trad. 8.

[351] *Man La Yahdharoh al-Faqih,* vol. 4, p. 275, ch. 176, trad. 10.

[352] *Mustadrak al-Wasa'il*, vol. 13, p. 46, ch. 16, trad. 5, narrating from *al-Ja'fariyyat* p. 155.

because it is a prerequisite to advancement. What is undesirable and objectionable, as referred to by this tradition, is to bank on wishes believing that wishes only will get you to your goal. What is objectionable is not to plan and work simply because you wish or hope that your wishes and goals will automatically be realized.

Resist Sleeping

The Commander of the Faithful Imam Ali (a) said:

> What a destroyer sleep is for [the fulfillment of] resolutions of the day.[353]

Sleep is a dangerous enemy to resolution and willpower to achieve one's goals. How many people were determined to achieve something but they did not because they favored sleeping and laziness over activity and work.

Imam Ali (a) also said:

> Woe unto the sleeper, what a failure he is! He shortened his life and his reward became reduced.[354]

The one who sleeps may miss obligations such as obligatory *jihad* (fighting in the way of God), enjoining the good and forbidding the evil. In this case, woe unto the sleeper, and he will be punished for that. If he sleeps and misses recommended deeds or work, or advancement opportunities, then it is as if woe is unto him.[355]

Imam Ali (a) also said:

> What a bad debtor (or opponent) is sleep, for it consumes the short life and causes one to miss out on a lot of good deeds.[356]

---

[353] *Nahj al-Balagha*, maxim 440.

[354] *Ghurar al-Hikam*, vol. 2, p. 303, ch. 83, trad. 30.

[355] This means that he did not commit a sin, but since he wasted time and missed opportunities, it is as if woe is unto him.

[356] *Ghurar al-Hikam*, vol. 1, p. 304, ch. 20, trad. 33.

Sleep is a silent monster which devours opportunities, consumes one's life, and deprives a person of rewards, so why surrender to it?

Make a Schedule for the Activities of the Day and Night

Imam Ali (a) says:

> The one who sleeps a lot at night will miss work which he will not be able to fulfill during the day.[357]

There are activities and programs for the night, and there are activities and programs for the day, and this varies according to societies or cultures. For example, the day can be for work and doing business, while the night can be for social relations and visiting others. If someone misses some night activities due to excessive sleeping, then one will usually not be able to fulfill them during the day time. If we assume that one can, then it will be done at the expense of the day time activities. The opposite also applies to the one who sleeps a lot during the day; but imagine about the one who sleeps a lot during both times?

Avoid Overeating

Imam Ali (a) says:

> Overeating and oversleeping corrupt the self (soul) and bring about harm.[358]

Overeating is considered among the factors which lead to the squandering of wealth and may also lead to poverty. Overeating is among the leading causes of diseases, illnesses and disorders, and overeating also squanders wealth due to the costs of treatment that it incurs. Furthermore, overeating weakens productivity, significantly and unnecessarily consumes food supplies, and on top of that, it is harmful. All of this, in the long

---

[357] Ibid., vol. 2, p. 216, ch. 77, trad. 1173.

[358] Ibid., vol. 2, p. 102, ch. 37, trad. 37.

run, leads to rising prices and higher living costs, because with higher demand, prices will also increase. It also often leads to the deprivation of many poor people from foods that are low in supply.

Seek Sustenance between Dawn and Sunrise

It has been narrated that the Commander of the Faithful Imam Ali (a) said in the *Hadith of the 400*:

> Seek sustenance between dawn and sunrise, for it is faster in delivering sustenance to you than traveling; and it is the hour in which Allah divides sustenance among His servants.[359]

One possible reason for that—in addition to the Divine factors—is that adrenaline, which is the hormone for liveliness and activity, surges in the body during this period. In addition, the human being experiences the peak of mental clarity between dawn and sunrise, and one is also calm and composed during that time. Therefore, one is able to plan better and make correct decisions.

It has been narrated that Imam Ali (a) said:

> Sleeping before sunrise and before the night (*isha'*) prayer brings about poverty and disorganization.[360]

The reason for this is because the period that precedes sunrise is a point of natural and physical transformation, just as it is a point of biological and psychological transformation in the human being.[361] The same applies to the period that precedes Ishaa' (which is about an hour or so after sunset).

During points of change or transformation, it is necessary to prepare onself with prayer and work. As for sleeping, it is an

---

[359] *Al-Khisaal*, vol. 2, p. 616, hadith no. 10, *Hadith of the 400.*

[360] *Mustadrak al-Wasa'il*, vol. 13, p. 110, ch. 31, trad. 2, narrating from the book *Hilya* by Allamah al-Majlisi, p. 126.

[361] The author has explained this in his book *Imam al-Husayn (a) and the Branches of Faith.*

escape from facing the needs and demands of that time. Thus, it brings about poverty and disorganization.

To conclude, Imam Ali (a) says:

> Spending this money in the obedience of Allah is the greatest blessing, and spending it in His disobedience is the biggest adversity.[362]

[362] *Ghurar al-Hikam*, vol. 1, p. 214, ch. 9, trad. 17.

The Richest Treasure

Introduction

Malik al-Ashtar was a famous companion of Imam Ali b. Abi Talib. He was the head of the Bani Nakha'i clan; a faithful disciple of Imam Ali b. Abi Talib; a brave warrior who acted as a Commander-in-Chief of the armies of Imam Ali b. Abi Talib; and his valour had earned him the title of the "Fearless Tiger".

Imam Ali b. Abi Talib had specially taught him the principles of administration and jurisprudence and he venerated and loved the Imam sincerely, and because of this, he earned Muawiya's exgtreme enmity.

Muawiya had conspired against him and had him killed by his gang of hirelings. His untimely death deeply grieved Imam Ali b. Abi Talib who expressing his grief said: "He was to me, what I was to the Noble Prophet."

The following instructions in the form of a letter was written to him by Imam Ali who appointed him as the Governor of Egypt in place of Muhammad b. Abi Bakr.

This letter is a précis of the principles of administration and justice as dictated by Islam. It deals with the duties and obligations of rulers, their chief responsibilities, the question of priorities of rights and obligations, dispensation of justice, control over secretaries and subordinate staff; distribution of work and duties amongst the various branches of administration, their co-ordination with each other and their co-operation within a center.

In it, Imam Ali advises Malik to combat corruption and oppression amongst the officers, to control markets, imports and exports, to curb evils of profiteering, hoarding, and black-marketing.

In it he has also explained stages of various classes in a society, the duties of the government towards the lowest class, how they are to be looked after and how their conditions are to be improved, the principle of equitable distribution of wealth and opportunities, orphans and their upbringing, maintenance of the handicapped, crippled and disabled people, and substitutes in lieu of homes for the aged and the disabled.

He then discusses the army, who it should consist of and how the ignorant, ruthless and corrupt mercenaries should not be allowed to join the army as their profession. He lays great stress upon the honour and nobility of volunteers who in time of need, offer their voluntary services to defend the flegling states governed by Islamic rule. Finally, he comments upon the rights of rulers over the ruled and of the ruled, over the rulers.

There is a main central idea running through all of these instructions, just like a single thread out of which a cloth is woven which is that of Allah. The regime is of Allah and the governors and the governed are both creatures of Allah, and their respective duties are laid down by Allah.

He expects each one of them to fulfill their obligations and perform their duties. The orphans and the depressed are a trust of Allah; the army is the army of Allah, and their soldiers should not behave like haughty and arrogant mercenaries, but like honorable and noble knights; everyone is expected to do their duty to the best of one's ability and through this, everyone will be rewarded in Paradise accordingly.

In short, this letter is on one hand, the Gospel of the principles of administration as taught by the Noble Quran, a code to establish a kind and benevolent rule, throwing light on various aspects of justice, benevolence and mercy, an order based on the ethics of Divine rulership where justice and mercy are shown to human beings irrespective of their class, creed and color where poverty is neither a stigma, nor a disqualification and where justice is not tainted with nepotism, favoritism, provincialism or religious fanaticism; and on the other hand, it is a thesis on the higher values of morality.

The famous Arab Christian, jurist, poet and philosopher Abdul Masih Antaki who died sometime in the beginning of the 20th Century, while discussing this letter writes that it is a far superior and better code than the one handed down by Moses and Hamurabi. It explains what a human administration should be like, how it should be carried out and it justifies the claims of Muslims that Islam wants to introduce a Divine administration of the people for the people by the people; and it wants a ruler to rule - not to please himself, but to bring happiness to the ruled. He notes that no religion before Islam tried to achieve this end and that Imam Ali b. Abi Talib should be congratulated for having introduced these principles during his rule, and for having written them down for the posterity.

۞ ۞ ۞

The Letter of Imam Ali to Malik al-Ashtar[363]

(Written when the Imam appointed him as the governor of Egypt and its regions, at a time when the rule of its governor, Muhammad b. Abi Bakr, was unstable; it is the longest of the letters written by the Imam, and the most all-embracing as regards to beauty of its form and the excellence of its meaning.)

In the Name of God, the Compassionate, the Merciful

This is what the servant of God, Ali, Commander of the Faithful, enjoined upon Malik b. al-Harith al-Ashtar, in his mandate to him, when he appointed him as governor of Egypt in order to

[363] Translated by Reza Shah-Kazmi

collect its revenues; to fight its enemies; to establish the welfare of its inhabitants; and to bring prosperity to its lands.

He enjoins him to have fear of God; to prefer obedience to God [above all things]; and to abide by what He has commanded in His Book - acts both obligatory and recommended - for no one prospers except through abiding by them, and no one is wretched except through repudiating and neglecting them. [He further enjoins him] to assist God with his heart, his hand and his tongue: for truly He - majestic is His Name - has undertaken to grant victory to the one who assists Him, and to elevate the one who exalts Him. He enjoins him to break the passionate desires of his soul, and to restrain it when it is beset with whim and caprice, for truly the soul incites to evil, unless God has mercy (upon that person).

Be aware Malik, that I am directing you to a land which has been ruled by states - just and unjust – before you; and that the people will evaluate your conduct, just as you have evaluated the conduct of the governors before you. They will speak about you just as you spoke about them; and the righteous are proven such only through what God has caused to flow from the tongues of His servants. So let your most beloved treasure be the treasure of virtuous acts. Dominate your inclinations, and exercise self-restraint in the face of that which is unlawful for you - for indeed self-restraint engenders within the soul a proper balance as regards to what it likes and what it dislikes.

Infuse your heart with mercy for the subjects, love for them and kindness towards them. Do not be like a ravenous beast of prey above them, seeking to devour them. For they are of two types: either your brother in religion or your like in creation. Mistakes slip from them, defects emerge from them, deliberately or accidentally. So bestow upon them your forgiveness and your pardon, just as you would like God to bestow upon you His forgiveness and pardon; for you are above them, and the one who has authority over you is above you, and God is above him who appointed you. He expects you to satisfy their needs; and through them He tests you.

Do not set your soul up for war with God. For before His retribution you have no resistance, and in the face of His forgiveness and mercy, (you have) no independence. So feel no regret when you pardon, and do not rejoice when you punish. Do not let an impulse propel you rashly towards any course of action, if you can see an alternative to it. Do not say, 'I have been given authority, and so my orders should be obeyed', for this leads to corruption in the heart and the erosion of religion; and it brings closer the adversities of fate. If the authority of your position engenders vanity and arrogance, then look at the grandeur of God's dominion above you, and at His power to do for you that which you have no power to do for yourself. This will calm your ambition, restrain you from your own vehemence, and restore to you what had strayed from your intellect. Beware of comparing [yourself] with God in greatness and likening (yourself) to Him in might, for God abases every tyrant and disgraces every arrogant one. Be just with God and be just with the people [giving them what is their due] from yourself, from your close relatives, and from those of your subjects towards whom you are most affectionate. If you fail to do this, then you will be an oppressor; and he who oppresses the servants of God will find that God, as well as His servants, will oppose him. God refutes the argument of whomever He opposes. He [the oppressor] remains at war with God until he desists and repents. Nothing so surely induces the removal of God's grace and hastens His retribution as persistence in oppression. For God hears the cry of the oppressed and keeps a vigilant watch over the oppressors.

Let the most beloved of affairs to you be those most centered upon the right, the most comprehensive in justice, and the most inclusive of popular contentment, for the discontent of the common folk undermines the contentment of the elite; while the discontent of the elite is compensated by the contentment of the common folk. In times of prosperity no subjects are more of a burden to the ruler as regards seeking his favour than the elite, and none who are less helpful to him in times of trial, none more repelled than they by justice, more persistent in making demands, less grateful when granted favour, slower to pardon when deprived, and less patient in the face of the vicissitudes of time. By contrast, the pillar of the religion, the cohesion of the Muslims, and the implement [for fighting] the enemies are constituted by the common folk, so be well disposed to them and incline towards them.

Let those of your subjects who most keenly seek out the faults of others be the ones furthest away from you and the most despicable in your eyes. For people do have faults which it behooves the governor - above all others - to conceal. So do not disclose those faults which remain hidden from you. Your duty is but to purify that which has become apparent and obvious to you; God will judge concerning those things which remain hidden from you. So try and veil deficiencies as much as you can, so that God may veil from your subjects that in yourself which you wish to be veiled. Untie the knot of all resentment amongst the people, and cut from yourself the rope of all rancour. Ignore everything which is obscure to you. Never be quick to believe a slanderer, for a slanderer is a deceiver, even if he appear in the guise of a good adviser.

Do not allow into your sphere of consultation any misers, for they will deflect you from generosity and threaten you with poverty; nor any cowards, for they will weaken you in your affairs; nor those who are avaricious, for they will adorn avidity for you with injustice.

Truly miserliness, cowardice and avarice are diverse inclinations comprised within a bad opinion of God. The worst of your ministers is one who ministered to evil (rulers) before you, and participated in their sins. So do not allow them to enter your inner circle, for they are assistants to sinners, and brothers of tyrants. The best alternative to them will be found among those who are as intelligent and capable as they are, but who are not saddled with their burden of sin, and have not assisted any tyrant in his tyranny, nor any sinner in his sin. Such people will be less of a burden for you in regards to provision, most helpful to you in regards to succor, most deeply inclined towards you in affection, and the least attached to people other than you. So choose such people as intimate companions, to be with you in private and in public. Within this group, give preference to one who most sincerely speaks the truth, however bitter it may be to you; and who supports you the least in doing that which God dislikes for His friends, however painfully this may strike at your desires.

Attach yourself to those who are known for their piety and sincerity, and train them in such a manner that they do not flatter you with lavish praise for doing something which you have not in fact done. For excessive praise breeds pride and carries one headlong towards vainglory. Do not place the virtuous and the wicked in the same rank before you, for this will result in the virtuous belittling the virtues and the wicked entrenching their vices. Impose upon them [the appropriate reward or punishment for] what they have imposed upon themselves. Be aware that nothing so effectively engenders the governor's confidence in his subjects other than his virtuous behaviour towards them, his relieving of their hardship, and his refraining from compelling them to do what is beyond their power.

Let there arise a situation in which you can enjoy confidence in your subjects, for such an attitude will spare you much trouble. He who is most worthy of your confidence is one by whom your trial was deemed good, while he who is most deserving of your distrust is one by whom your trial was deemed bad.

Do not rupture any beneficial tradition that was established by the leaders of the community, as a result of which unity has been harmoniously established, and from which the subjects have prospered. Do not set a new practice which is detrimental to the already established traditions for if you do so, then the reward for their observance will rebound to him who established them, while the onus of their destruction will be upon you.

Study a lot with the scholars and hold many discourses with the sages, in order to consolidate that which brings well-being to your lands, and to further entrench that which has already been established by your predecessors. Be aware that the subjects consist of various classes, none of which can be sound without the others being so, and none can function independently from the others. Among these classes are the soldiers of God; the scribes - administering to the common people and the elite; the judges - officials responsible for upholding fairness, and establishing the right of redress; those who pay the jizya (poll-tax) and the kharaj (land-tax) from among the 'protected people' (ahl al-dhimma) and the Muslims; the merchants and artisans; and the lowest class – comprising of the needy and the destitute. God has prescribed to each [class] its share and has ordained - as a binding covenant with us from Him - for each of its limits and its duties, according to His Book or the Sunnah (tradition) of the Prophet - may God bless him and his family.

So as regards to the soldiers, they are - by the grace of God - the fortresses of the subjects, the adornment of the governors, the power of religion, and the pathways to security. The subjects cannot maintain themselves except by means of the soldiers, and the soldiers for their part cannot be maintained except by means of the [revenues of the] kharaj which God extracts for them; with this, they have the means to wage war on their enemies, establish their welfare, and fulfill their needs.

These two classes [the soldiers and the peasants] cannot be maintained except through a third: the judges, administrators and scribes, inasmuch as they uphold all of the contracts, harmonize and organize all interests and benefits, being charged with the maintenance of the specific and general affairs [of state and society]. All of these classes need for their proper functioning the merchants and artisan, who gather the requisite goods, and establish the appropriate markets. They fulfill [the needs of the other classes] by procuring through their specific functions those resources which cannot be obtained by the work of others. Finally, there is the lowest class, consisting of the needy and the destitute -those deserving assistance and favour. For each [class] there is plenitude with God; and each has, in relation to the governor, a right proportioned to the needs of its welfare. The governor cannot fully accomplish the tasks imposed upon him by God without resolute determination and resorting to God's help, galvanizing himself for the prerogatives of rectitude, and manifesting patience in the face of ease and difficulty.

Appoint as the commander of your soldiers a person whom you deeply feel is the most sincere in his relation to God, the Prophet and your Imam, the purest of heart, the one most excellent in forbearance, one who is not so fast to get angry, happy to pardon, kind to the weak, severe with the strong, one who is neither moved by violence, nor held back by weakness. Cleave to those of noble descent, belonging to pious families of established name and repute, and to men known for their bravery, courage, generosity and tolerance - for they constitute a group formed by nobility, and a party made of honour. Then supervise their affairs as parents would supervise their children. Let no act by which you strengthen them appear too great in your eyes. Do not belittle any kindness - however slight - which you have promised them, for such kindness is as a summoner unto them, calling them to dispense good advice to you, and to enjoin trust in you. Do not abandon a close inspection of their affairs in favour of [ostensibly more] weighty matters, for there may be a situation in which they benefit from even a small act of kindness, and one in which they cannot dispense with the weighty matters.

Let the most preferred of your commanders be the one who is more benevolent to the people, and most generous to them with his bounty, such that they have ample means, both the people and those among their relatives who succeed them. Let their concern be integrated within one resolve: to fight the enemy. Know that your kindness towards them will cause their hearts to incline towards you.

The greatest source of joy for the governors is the establishment of justice in the land, and the emanation of love from his subjects. Such love will not be manifest unless their hearts are secure. Their advice will not be sound except through the governors' supervision of those in charge of the subjects' affairs, and that they ensure to find the burden of rule light and easy to bear, and that they no longer anxiously hope that the rule of the governor will be terminated. So raise their hopes, keep up your continuous praise of them, and your enumeration of the brave deeds of those who have been brave - for truly, abundant praise of their noble acts rouse the brave, and spur on the lazy, if God wills. Acknowledge the courageous deeds of every man, and do not ascribe the deeds of one person to someone else, or fall short in granting due acknowledgement. Do not let the nobility of a man cause you to reckon a small accomplishment as great; and do not allow the lowliness of a man cause you to reckon (a great accomplishment of his as) small.

Refer to God and His Messenger in any matter which weighs heavily on you, or which is unclear to you, for God the Exalted has declared to a folk whom He loved to guide: "O you who believe, obey God and obey the Messenger and those in authority among you; and if you dispute with one another over anything, then refer it to God and the Messenger."[364] To 'refer to God' means following that which is clear and unequivocal in His Book; and 'refer to the Messenger' means following that part of his Sunnah (tradition) which unites, rather than that which divides.

Choose as judges those whom you consider the most excellent of your subjects - those who are not confused by complex matters, nor angered by disputants; who do not persist in error, and are not restrained about turning to the truth when they perceive it; whose souls are not susceptible to avarice; those who when they are dissatisfied with a superficial understanding, will probe

[364] *Quran*, Surah al-Nisa (4), verse 59.

deeply; who are most cautious in the face of ambiguities; most consequent in argumentation; least perturbed by the appeals of litigants; most patient in efforts to disclose the true state of affairs; most resolute when the right judgement is clear; who are not beguiled by praise, nor misled by blandishment. Such people are indeed rare!

Then examine carefully and frequently the execution of the judge's verdicts, and be generous in paying him, so that any deficiency [in terms of livelihood] will be removed, thus diminishing his need for help from the people. Bestow upon him a rank of proximity to yourself, one which nobody else from among your close companions might hope to attain. He should be made safe in your presence and be protected against the attacks of other influential men. Scrutinize them with a piercing scrutiny, for this religion has been held captive in the hands of evil people, abused by them and their caprice, exploited by them for the sake of this world.

Now consider your administrators. Employ them after due examination, and do not appoint them out of any partiality or favouritism for such indulgence will engender various forms of injustice and treachery. Look for men of proven experience and modesty from among the righteous households, families enjoying precedence in Islam, for they are the most noble in character, most rooted in dignity, least susceptible to greedy desires, and more acutely conscious of the consequences of all things. Provide them with a generous stipend, for this will be a source of strength for them, enabling them to establish their welfare, obviating any need to appropriate for themselves what they have power over, and providing an argument against them should they disobey your orders or betray your trust. Examine carefully their actions, by appointing supervisors known for their sincerity and reliability to watch over them. Your secret observation of their affairs will motivate them to fulfill their trust, and to be considerate towards the subjects. Pay attention also to your assistants: should any one of them stretch his hand towards some treacherous deed - and your observers are unanimous in their report, which you deem sufficient evidence of the act - then impose corporal punishment upon him. Let him be chastised on account of the affliction caused by his act. Let him be disgraced, brand him as a traitor, and gird him with the ignominy of accusation.

Carefully examine the question of the *kharaj*, so that those subject to it are maintained in a proper state of well-being, for it is from their welfare, and the proper collection of the tax itself, that the benefit of others is derived. There can be no welfare of others except through them [the peasants], for everyone without exception is dependent upon the [revenues of the] kharaj and those subject to it. Let your concern with the cultivation of the land outweigh your concern with the collection of the tax, for no tax will be collected if there is no cultivation; and whoever exacts the tax, without cultivating the land, ruins the land and destroys the people. His rule will not endure for long.

So if they complain about a heavy burden - or about some deficiency or the cutting of irrigation supplies, or lack of rain, or a change in the condition of the soil as a result of flooding or drought - then lighten their burden, inasmuch as your hope is that their situation be set right. Do not let any favour that you bestow upon them - by way of lightening their burden - weigh heavily upon you; for this will be an investment, which will yield a return for you in terms of the prosperity of your land and the adornment of your rule, through your reaping the finest praise from them, and taking pride in dispensing justice among them. You can then expect an increase in their potential as a result of what you have invested in them when you gave them respite; and you can trust them inasmuch as you have accustomed them to receiving your justice and kindness.

It is possible that a situation may arise in which you depend upon them: and they will then bear this responsibility gladly, for a prosperous land can bear a burden which you place upon it. The devastation of the land only comes about through the destitution of its inhabitants; and the destitution of its inhabitants only comes about when the desire to amass wealth rules the souls of the governors, when they have doubts about what endures, and when they profit little from exemplary teachings.

Now consider with care the situation of your scribes, appointing the best of them in charge of your affairs. Assign those letters containing the most sensitive strategies and secrets to the scribe in whom you find the most comprehensive moral qualities; one who will not be emboldened by his elevated status to contradict you in the presence of others at a public assembly; one who is not negligent in delivering to you the correspondence of your officials, and properly despatching your replies, regarding what he takes and gives on your behalf. He must not weaken any agreement contracted for you, nor be incapable of repudiating that which has been contracted to your detriment. He must not be ignorant about the value of his own capabilities; for one who is unaware of the value of his own capabilities will be even more ignorant to the value of others. Do not allow yourself to make your selection only on the basis of your own discrimination, confidence and trust, for men know how to present themselves to the discrimination of rulers through pretence and good service, behind which there is no sincerity or fidelity. Rather, investigate them carefully, doing so in relation to that with which they were entrusted with by good people before you; and (put your) trust in one whose virtue left the deepest impression upon the common people, and whose reputation for integrity is the most widespread. This will be proof of your sincerity towards God and towards the one who appointed you.

Appoint for each of your affairs a head-officer among your officials, one who will not be daunted by the magnitude of affairs nor dispersed by their multiplicity. Any fault of your scribes which you have ignored will be ascribed to yourself.

Then attend to the merchants and artisans. Treat them well, urging the same on others. [Among them are] those of fixed abode, those who travel with their goods, and those who earn their livelihood with their own hands. They are sources of benefit and the means by which conveniences are obtained. By them are procured goods from distant and remote places, brought by land and sea, from plains and mountains, and from places where men do not settle nor even dare to venture. They are in a state of reconciliation, and from them no calamity needs to be feared; and they are in a state of peace, from them no disturbance needs to be feared. Examine their affairs attentively, both those which are close to you and those in all corners of your land. Be aware that, despite what has been said, there is in many of them a despicable stinginess, a repugnant greed, a propensity to hoard goods, and to arbitrarily fix prices. All of this brings about loss for the populace, and is a source of shame for the governors. So prohibit hoarding, for the Messenger of God - God bless him and his family - prohibited it. Let trading be carried out with propriety and fairness, according to prices which do not harm either of the two parties; the buyers or the sellers. So if any one of them succumb to the temptation to hoard, after you have prohibited it, then inflict upon him an exemplary punishment - but not too excessive.

Then – O God, O God! - [pay particular attention to] the lowest class, those who have no means, the destitute, the needy, the afflicted, the disabled. Within this class are those who beg, and those whose wretchedness calls out to be alleviated but do not beg. Be mindful of God in regards to their rights, for He has entrusted these rights to your care. Assign to them a portion from your public treasury, and a portion of the produce of what is taken as booty by the Muslims in every region, for those who are furthest have the same rights as those who are nearer. Upholding the right of each of them is incumbent upon you. Do not let any haughtiness on your part cause you to neglect them, for you will not be pardoned even the slightest shortcoming [in fulfilling your obligations towards them] as a result of attending to some important matter. So do not turn your concern away from them, nor assume a contemptuous attitude towards them.

Keep a watchful eye over the affairs of those who have no access to you, and who are disdained by men of high standing. Appoint from among those whom you trust a God-fearing and humble person to be responsible for bringing their affairs to your attention. Treat these people in a manner such that God may excuse you on the day you will meet Him, for they are more in need of justice from you than anyone else from among your subjects. In regard to each of them, offer your excuse to God in respect of fulfilling his right. Assume responsibility for the orphans and the elderly, those who have no resources yet cannot bring themselves to beg. This is difficult for the governors, and [the fulfillment] of all rights is tiring, but God makes it light for those who aspire for the Hereafter, who restrain their souls in patience, and trust in the truth of that which is promised to them by God.

Apportion a part of your time for those who have special needs, making yourself free to attend to them personally, sitting with them in a public assembly with all due humility before God, your Creator. Keep your soldiers, guards and officers away from them, so that they can speak to you in an uninhibited manner, for I heard the Messenger of God say - God bless him and his family - on more than one occasion: 'A nation in which the rights of the weak are not wrested in an uninhibited manner from the strong will never be blessed.'

Bear patiently any coarseness or inarticulate expression that they might manifest; do not show any irritation or disdain towards them – God will thereby extend the most extensive dimensions of His compassion to you and make incumbent the reward for your obedience to Him. Give whatever you give with beneficence, and withhold [if this be unavoidable] with grace and apology.

There are certain affairs which you must take care of personally – among which are replying to your officers if your scribes are incapable of doing so; issuing [responses to] the requests of people when they are brought to you in person because your aides find their hearts constricted on their account.

Each day, perform the job that is appropriate for it, for to each day belongs a particular task. Set apart the most excellent of your available time, and the greatest portions thereof, for your soul, for what is between you and God, even though every time [and actions performed therein] are for God, if the intention underlying them is good, and if your subjects derive security as a consequence. Let your observance of those duties relating exclusively to God be the special means by which you purify your religion for God. Give to God from your vital energy in your nights and your days, and perform fully that which will draw you nearer to God, doing so perfectly, without becoming dull or deficient, taking your body to its limits.

When you lead the people in prayer, do so without repelling [them] or squandering [it], for there are people with infirmities or special needs. Indeed, I asked the Messenger of God - God bless him and his family - when he sent me [as his representative] to Yemen. 'How should I lead them in prayer?' He replied, 'Lead them according to the prayer performed by the weakest among them; and be merciful to the believers.'

In addition to all of this, do not prolong any period of absence from your subjects, for the isolation of the governors from their subject, is a kind of constriction and causes deficiency in awareness of their affairs. Such isolation will cut the rulers off from acquiring knowledge about things hidden from them, so that which is great will appear small, and that which is small will appear to be great; the beautiful will appear ugly, and the ugly, beautiful; and the truth will be mixed up with the falsehood. The governor is but a human being: he does not know what the people hide from him. There are no visible signs on the truth, by virtue of which apparent expressions of veracity can be distinguished from falsehood.

You can only be one of two types: either a man who gives himself generously for the sake of the truth - in which case why seclude yourself [thereby preventing yourself] from bestowing a necessary right or performing an honourable deed? Or else you are a man afflicted with refusal [to give of oneself] in which case, how quickly people will refrain from making requests to you, despairing of your generosity!

This, despite the fact that [fulfilling] most of the needs which people present to you is not burdensome, whether they be complaints against injustice or demands for fairness in transactions.

The governor has favourites and intimate friends, among whom some are prone to presumptuousness, arrogance and unfairness in transactions. Sever the root of these people by eliminating the causes of these vices, by not allotting any landed estates to anyone among your entourage or friends. Do not let them entertain any hope that you may grant them some estate; [were they to receive such an estate] it would be detrimental for those living adjacent to it, as regards [their access to] water resources, or any common undertaking, the burden of which would without doubt fall upon them, while the profit from there would redound to those acquiring the estate, and not upon you. Upon you will fall only the resulting blame, both in this world and in the next.

Impose what is right upon whomsoever it is incumbent, whether that person be close to you or distant. Be steadfast and vigilant in this matter, regardless of how it may affect your close ones and favourites. Always desire the consequences of [this principle], however heavily it may weigh upon you, for its outcome will be laudable.

If any of your subjects suspect you of an injustice, present your case such that you may be exonerated, thus deflecting their suspicions away from you through your clear explanations. Such conduct is a means of self-discipline, it is a form of kindness towards your subjects, and a way of presenting your plea which will help you fulfill your need to keep them upright in accordance with the truth.

Never reject any call to peace made to you by your enemy,

if there be divine acceptance of his call, for truly in peace lies repose for your soldiers, relaxation of your concerns, and security for your lands. But maintain all due vigilance regarding your enemies once you have contracted peace with them, for it is possible that the enemy is only making peace with you in order to lull you into a false sense of security. So proceed with all due precaution, and be wary of having too much of a trusting opinion in such circumstances. But if you and your enemy enter into a solemn agreement, or if he obtains from you the right of protection, then faithfully abide by what you have promised, and honourably uphold your obligation of protection. Make your very life a shield for what you have promised, for there is no divine obligation which so strongly unites people - despite having diverse inclinations and multifarious opinions - like that of honouring the principle of fulfilling one's pledge. The polytheists had observed this amongst themselves - even apart from their dealings with the Muslims - such was their dread of the consequences of treachery. So do not violate your pledge of protection, do not break your promises, and do not be treacherous towards your enemy - for only an ignorant wretch dares to oppose God. God has indeed made His pledge and His protection a means of security, spreading it over His servants by His mercy, a sanctuary in the impregnability by which they find peace, and towards the protective power of which they make haste. So let there be no corruption, no treachery, and no deception. Do not enter into any agreement which contains defects, nor fall back on ambiguous connotations once the agreement has been confirmed and solemnized. Do not let any difficult matter lead you to break unfairly an agreement which God has made binding upon you. For indeed, your patience in the face of a difficulty - hoping for its resolution and positive outcome is better than acting treacherously and then fearing its consequences: being overwhelmed by an exacting demand from God, from which you will not be able to seek exemption in this life or in the next.

Beware of unlawfully shedding blood: nothing is more

conducive to retribution, more momentous in consequence, more deserving of the cessation of blessings and the severance of one's term than the unjust shedding of blood. On the Day of Resurrection, God - glorified be He – will commence judgement of His servants by [calling them to account over] the blood that they had shed. So do not try to strengthen your authority by unlawful bloodshed, for such action in fact weakens and debilitates it indeed and will bring it to an end and will remove you (from the authority).

You have no excuse before God or before me if you intentionally murder anyone, for this calls forth capital punishment. If you fall prey to some error, and your tongue or your hand goes too far in inflicting a punishment - for even a punch, or other such assaults can be a cause of death - do not allow pride in your power to make you seek a way of avoiding payment of what is rightfully due as recompense to the relatives of the person killed.

Beware of being self-satisfied, of being over-confident in what you find impressive about yourself, or loving to be flattered, for these are among Satan's most reliable opportunities to efface the virtue of the virtuous. Beware of making your subjects beholden to you for your virtue towards them; of exaggerating Your deeds; or making promises to them which you will break. For making people beholden ruins virtue; exaggeration removes the light of truth; and breaking promises imposes upon you the hatred of God and men. God the Exalted has said: 'It is indeed hateful to God that you say that which you do not do'.[365] Beware of rushing your affairs before their proper time, of squandering the possibility of dealing with them, obstinacy when they prove intractable, or of feebleness in dealing with them when they become manifestly clear. Put every affair in its proper place, and deal with it in its proper time. Beware of appropriating that in which all men have an equal share, and of negligence in regards to what is urgent and has become self-evident, for this will be to

---

[365] *Quran*, Surah al-Saff (61), verse 3.

the detriment of yourself, and to the benefit of others. Soon, the veil covering all of the affairs will be lifted for you, and justice will be sought from you by those who have been wronged.

Dominate the zeal of your pride, the vehemence of your castigation, the power of your hand, and the sharpness of your tongue. Guard against these vices by restraining all impulsiveness, and putting off all resort to force until your anger subsides, and you regain self-control. But you cannot attain such self-domination without increasing your pre-occupation with remembrance of your return to your Lord.

It is incumbent upon you to remember what transpired in earlier times in regards to the just rules and virtuous customs, the practices of the Prophet - God bless him and his family - and the obligations enshrined in the Book of God. So faithfully follow that which you have witnessed us performing in these respects, and strive with all of your soul to act in accordance with the injunctions contained in this mandate of mine. I am confident that this [mandate] will furnish an argument for myself against you, so you will have no excuse if your soul hastens instead to gratify its caprice. I beseech God by the abundance of His compassion, and the magnitude of His power, to fulfill every desire, to cause me and you to do that which will please Him, to present a clear justification to Him and His creatures, to earn the fairest praise amongst the servants [of God], and to leave behind us the most beautiful vestiges in the land. [I beseech Him to grant us] perfect blessings and an ever-increasing honour, and that He seal [the lives of] myself and yourself with felicity and the testimony, 'And truly back to Him we are returning.'[366]

Peace be upon the Messenger of God - God bless him and his good and pure progeny.

---

366 *Quran*, Surah al-Baqarah (2), verse 156.

Other books by the Author (Arabic)

1. Shedding Light on the Life of Imam Ali (a).
2. Shura al-Fuqaha' (Council of the Jurists), a legal and jurisprudential work.
3. Rays from the Light of Fatima al-Zahra (a), a study on the essential value of loving Fatima (a).
4. Lady Narjes (a): A School for the Generations.
5. Discussions on Creed and Conduct: A series of lectures based on Quran verses delivered at the Zaynabiyya Seminary and also in the holy city of Najaf.
6. Intellectual Dialogue.
7. Shedding Light on Tawalli and Tabarri.
8. Lessons on Usul al-Kafi, the first section, the Book of Intellect and Ignorance.
9. The Law of Cooperation on Righteousness and Piety.
10. Legislative and Advisory Commands (Jurisprudential work).
11. Al-Hujjah: Its Meanings and Applications.
12. Conceptual and Confirmatory Principles for Islamic Law and Legal Theory

13. A Study on the Parts of Sciences and their Components.
14. The Legitimacy, Sanctity, and Significance of Imam Husayn's (a) Revolution.
15. Be with the Truthful, exegetical discussions on the holy verse "Be with the Truthful."
16. Why Isn't the Name of Imam Ali (a) Explicitly Mentioned in the Noble Quran?
17. Main Guiding Principles that Guarantee Correctness in Intellectual Laws.
18. The Relativity of Texts and Knowledge: The Possible and Impossible.
19. A Critique of Hermeneutics and the Relativity of Truth, Knowledge, and Language.
20. From the Life of Imam Hasan (a).
21. The Law of Khums – Jurisprudential lessons delivered at the Zaynabiyya Seminary.
22. Legal Theory: The Discussion of Certainty (Qat'), two volumes.
23. The Explicit Mention of Imam Ali's Name in the Quran.
24. The Law of Jurisprudence and Emulation – Jurisprudential lessons delivered at the Seminary of Najaf.
25. A Discussion of the Law of Ilzaam - Jurisprudential lessons delivered at the Seminary of Najaf.
26. The Law of Illegal Transactions – Keeping the Books of Deviance and those that Cause Corruption.
27. Ijtihad in Usul al-Deen
28. Imam Husayn (a) and the Branches of Faith, a study on the strong relationship between the Master of Martyrs and every branch of the branches of faith.

29. The Strategies of Producing Wealth and Combating Poverty in the System of Imam Ali (This book which has been translated to English).
30. The Features of the Relationship between the State and the People.
31. The Features of a Civil Society in Islamic Thought.
32. Repent to Allah.
33. A Commentary on Du'a al-Iftitah.
34. The Dividing Line between Religions and Civilizations.
35. Who Commands the Highest Authority?
36. The Authenticity of the Marasil al-Thoqat (The Hurried Reports of Reliable Narrators) - [The Marasil of al-Saduq and al-Tousi as an example].
37. The Jurisprudence of the Objectives of the Shari'a.
38. The Law of Dreams, a discussion on the lack of authenticity of dreams based on the Quran, the Sunna, reason and knowledge.
39. Being Steadfast during the Era of Occultation.
40. Having Suspicious Doubts in Quranic Societies.
41. The Law of Illegal Transactions – the Law of Bribery.
42. The Law of the Exceptions of Lying.
43. The Law of Dealing with Counterfeit Money and Fraudulent Products.
44. Selective Emulation
45. The Law of Illegal Transactions – The Impermissibility of Aimless Play and Amusement.
46. The Jurisprudence of Innuendos and Double Entendre
47. Emulation in the Principles of Jurisprudence
48. Manifestations of Divine Support for the Blessed Zahra.

49. The Enlightenment of Revelation in Imamate (Divinely-Appointed Leadership)
50. The Law of Illegal Transactions – Discussions on Tattling.
51. Emulation of the Most Knowing.
52. A Critique of Some Philosophical and Mystical Principles.
53. Introductory Discussions on the Law of Rights.
54. Legal Theory: al-Hukuma wal Wurud.
55. The Book of Buying/Selling.
56. The Book of Contradicitions.
57. Introduction to the Science of Creed: A Critique of the Theory of Perception.
58. The Origins and Causes of Deviance.
59. Lessons from the Maxims of Nahj al-Balagha.

List of Sources

1. *Holy Quran*
2. *Nahj al-Balagha*
3. *Al-Ihtijaj* by al-Tabarsi; published by Matabe' al-No'man in Najaf, 1386 AH.
4. *Ihqaq al-Haqq wa Izhaq al-Batil*, by al-Qadhi Noorollah al-Husayni al-Mar'ashi al-Tostari, who was martyred in India in the year 1019; published by the Library of Mar'ashi al-Najafi in Qum, Iran.
5. *Irshad al-Qulub*, by al-Daylami; published by Manshoorat al-Radhi, Qum.
6. *Asbab al-Nuzul*, by al-Wahidi al-Naysabouri; published by Alhalabi Institute and Co.
7. *A'lam al Deen fi Sifat al-Mo'mineen*, by al-Daylami; published by Alulbayt Institue, Qum.
8. *Imam Al-Mahdi (a)*, by Sayed Mohammad Husayni al-Shirazi.
9. *Bihar al-Anwar* by al-Majlisi, published by Al-Wafa' Institute in Beirut, Lebanon, 1982.
10. *Tafsir al-Baydhawi*; published by Dar al-Fikr, Beirut.
11. *Tafsir al-Ayyashi*, by al-Samarqandi al-Ayyashi; published by al-Maktabah al-Ilmiyyah al-Islmaiyya, Tehran.

12. *Tafsir al-Kabir lil Fakhr al-Razi*, third edition.

13. *Tanbih al-Khawater wa Nuzhat al-Nawadher*, by Abil Husayn Warram al-Maliki al-Ashtari; published by Dar al-Kotob al-Islamiyyah, second edition, year 1368 AH.

14. *Tawdhih Nahj al-Balagha*, by Mohammad Al-Husayni al-Shirazi; published by Dar al-Ulum, Beirut, Lebanon, first edition, 2002.

15. *Tahdhib al-Ahkam*, by al-Tousi, third edition, 1364 AH, Tehran.

16. *Jame' Ahadith al-Shia*, by Sayed Husayn al-Boroujerdi; published by al-Matba'ah al-Ilmiyya, 1399 AH, Qum.

17. *Hukumat al-Rasoul (a) wal Imam Amirul Mu'mineen (a).*

18. *Al-Khisaal*, by Ibn Babawayh al-Qummi; published by Jama'at al-Modarressin of the Seminary of Qum, 1403 AH.

19. *Al-Khelaaf*, by al-Tousi, published by al-Nashr al-Islami Institute, 1407 AH.

20. *Al-Durr al-Manthour fil Tafsiri bil Ma'thour*, by Jalal al-Din al-Suyuti; along with the Tafsir of Ibn Abbas; published by Dar al-Ma'rifah, Beirut, Lebanon.

21. *Da'aem al-Islam*, by Abu Hanifah al-Tamimi al-Maghribi; published by Dar al-Ma'aref of Egypt, 1963.

22. *Dhakha'er al-Oqbah*, by Ahmad Ibn Abdullah al-Tabari; published the Qudsi Library.

23. *Rawa'e' Nahj al-Balagha*, by George Jordac, published by Markaz al-Ghadeer lil Dirasat al-Islamiyyah, third edition, 1417 AH.

24. *Rawdhatol Wa'idhin*, by al-Naysabouri; published by Manshoorat al-Radhi, Qum.

25. *Al-Siyasah min Waqi' al-Islam*, by Sayed Sadiq al-Husayni al-Shirazi; published by Yase Zahra, Qum, second edition, 1431

AH.

26. *Sharh Ihqaq al-Haq*, by Sayed al-Mar'ashi; published by Manshoorat Maktabat al-Sayed al-Mar'ashi al-Najafi, Qum.

27. *Sharh Risalat al-Huquq lil Imam Zayn al-Abidin (a)*, edited by Sayed Ali al-Qobbanchi, third edition, 1406 AH; published by Isma'ilian, Qum.

28. *Sharh Nahj al-Balagha*, by Ibn Abil Hadid; published by Dar Ihya' al-Koton al-Arabiyya, first edition, 1959.

29. *Shawahed al-Tanzil*, by al-Hakem al-Hasakani; published by Majma' Ihya' al-Thaqafah al-Islamiyya, first edition, 1411 AH, Tehran, Iran.

30. *Al-Siyaghah al-Jadidah*, by Sayed Mohammad al-Husayni al-Shirazi.

31. *Al-Dhaman al-Ijtima'i fil Islam*, by Sayed Sadiq al-Husayni al-Shirazi.

32. *Awali al-Li'ali*, by Ibn Abi Jomhour al-Ahsa'i, first edition, 1403 AH; published by Sayed al-Shohada Publications, Qum, Iran.

33. *Kitab al-Ayn*, by al-Farahidi; published by Dar al-Hijra Institute, second edition in Iran, 1409 AH.

34. *Uyun al-Akhbar al-Ridha (a)*, by al-Sadouq; published by al-A'lami Institute, Beirut, Lebanon, 1984.

35. *Ghurar al-Hikam*, by al-Amodi; published by Dar al-Hadi, first edition, 1992.

36. *Fatima al-Zahra (a) Afdhal Oswa lil Nisa'*, by Sayed Mohammad al-Husayni al-Shirazi.

37. *Fadha'el al-Khamsa minal Sehah al-Sitta*, by Sayed Mortadha al-Husayni al-Firouzabadi; by al-A'lami Institute, Beirut, Lebanon, second edition.

38. *Al-Fiqh al-Idarah*, by Sayed Mohammad al-Husayni al-Shirazi;

published by Dar al-Uloum, Beirut, 1992.

39. *Al-Fiqh al-Iqtisaad*, Sayed Mohammad al-Husayni al-Shirazi, published by Dar al-Uloum, Beirut, Lebanon, 1992, fifth edition.

40. *Al-Fiqh al-Dawlah al-Islamiyyah*, by Sayed Mohammad al-Husayni al-Shirazi.

41. *Al-Fiqh al-Awlamah*, by Sayed Mohammad al-Husayni al-Shirazi.

42. *Al-Fiqh al-Qadha'*, by Sayed Mohammad al-Husayni al-Shirazi.

43. *Al-Fiqh al-Morour*, by Sayed Mohammad al-Husayni al-Shirazi.

44. *Fi Sahihatel Amaleqah* by Jajer and Ortiz.

45. *Qorb al-Isnaad*, by al-Hemyari; published by Alulbayt Institute, first edition, 1413 AH, Qum.

46. *Al-Qarn al-Hadi wal Ishroon wa Tajdid al-Hayat*, by Sayed Mohammad al-Husayni al-Shirazi.

47. *Al-Kafi*, by al-Kulayni; published by Dar al-Kotob al-Islamiyyah, Tehran, third edition, 1388 AH.

48. *Kanzol Fawa'ed*, by Abil Fath al-Karajaki, second edition; published by Ghadeer, Qum.

49. *Lisan al-Arab*, by Ibn Mandhour Al-Ifriqi al-Misri; published by Adab al-Hawzah, Qum, Iran.

50. *Al-Mojatam' al-Arabi al-Mo'aser fil Qarnel Ishrin*, by Hakim Barakat; published by Markaz Dirasat al-Wahda al-Arabiyya, first edition, Beirut, 2000.

51. *Majma' al-Bahrain*, by al-Toraihi, revised by Mahmoud Adel; published by Naser Serow, second edition, 1983, Tehran.

52. *Majma' al-Bayan fi Tafsir al-Quran*, by al-Tabarsi, published by al-A'lami Institute, Beirut, first edition, 1415 AH.

53. *Mostadrak al-Wasa'il*, by Mirza Hossein al-Nouri al-Tabarsi; edited by Alulbayt Institute, first edition, Beirut, 1987.

54. *Mustadrak Safinat al-Bihar*, by Sheikh Ali Namazi Shahroudi; published by al-Nashr al-Islami Institute, Qum.

55. *Ma'alem al-Mojtama' al-Madani fi Mandhoomatel Fikril Islami*, by the author.

56. *Makarem al-Akhlaaq*, by Hasan Ibn Fadhl al-Tabarsi, sixth edition, 1987.

57. *Man La Yahdharah al-Faqih*, by al-Saduq; published by Jamiat al-Mudarrisin fil Hawza al-Ilmiyya, Qum, second edition.

58. *Manaqeb Ali Ibn Abi Talib (a)*, by Ibn al-Maghazili; published by Intisharat Sibtil Nabi (s), first edition, 1426 AH.

59. Al-Nabaa Information Network.

60. The website of Imam Shirazi World Institute for Studies, Washington, DC www.siironline.org

61. Wikipedia.com.

62. Arabic CNN.

63. Worldbank.org.

64. *Mohaj al-Da'awat wa Manhaj al-Ibadat*, by Sayed Ibn Tawoos; published by Sana'i Library.

65. *Wasa'il al-Shia*, by al-Hurr al-Amili; published by Alulbayt Institute, Qum, second edition, 1414 AH.

Advance Praise for *Economic Success*

I found this valuable book to be one of the best compilations in the field of Islamic economy. Throughout his exquisite book, the author examines various methods in combating poverty from an Islamic aspect.

The author's diagnosis for the most important challenge of our era—poverty—forms a considerable aspect of this book. Before providing any solutions, this recognition by itself reveals the author's deep insight into the perils of pervasive poverty.

Moral solutions along with economic ones provide a multi-dimensional package for resolving the global crisis of poverty. By focusing particularly on the era of Ali Ibn Abi Talib, the successor to Prophet Muhammad, Sayed Mortadha al-Husayni al-Shirazi attempts to legitimize the concept of what is called the "welfare state" as a solution for combating poverty. Without any doubt, this is a great contribution to enhance our understanding on Islam and its ideology.

Furthermore, the book provides a fairly unique understanding of wealth and poverty. Despite the misconception that Islam encourages poverty and asceticism, this book introduces a new idea about Islam's ethical vision of the concept of "wealth."

This paradigm shift in examining poverty and wealth is a revolutionary reform in the social values and ethics that commonly are ascribed to Islam; this is very similar to what happened to Christianity when protestants proposed their theory about the important role of being wealthy as a way to being closer to the Lord and as a sign of being a good believer.

Further development of the ideas which have been proposed in the book could elevate it to the level of being an important reference on Islam's vision for building a more just economic system.

-Scott Wakeman

Visiting Professor of "Islamic Finance" at Ohio University College of Business and Senior advisor in the Department of Middle Eastern Studies at Northern Finance Group, NFG.

I believe this book offers a unique interpretation of Islamic approaches to address poverty. The author describes the principles of Islamic economy and introduces us to an Islamic framework for social welfare. The author's merit of elicitation has inspired me to learn more about the social aspects of Islamic ideology as well as better understand the philosophies that have shaped these ideals. I also hope to explore the relationship between different schools of philosophy within the Islamic social framework.

-John J. Elton

Professor in the Department of Economics at Eastern Michigan University

www.ingramcontent.com/pod-product-compliance
Lightning Source LLC
Chambersburg PA
CBHW071548200326
41519CB00021BB/6648
* 9 7 8 0 9 9 1 0 2 5 0 2 2 *